Waldemar Góralski

The Japanese Battleship Kirishima 1940

In memory of my late friend Piotr Wiśniewski (†) to whom I am grateful for all the texts he wrote for my books.

KAGERO

Starboard side view.

In 1902, Japan signed an Alliance Pact with Britain, which was then a leading sea power. It ordered modern ships at British shipyards, and Japanese shipyards were to co-operate. After the new class of battlecruisers had emerged, Japan decided to design them for its navy. They were to be ships with a displacement of 19,000 tons and a main armament of 305 mm calibre guns. However, with the news that the British were working on a new design of the LION class cruiser with 343 mm main armament, work on the Japanese project was discontinued. An agreement was signed with the Vickers shipyard for the design and construction of new ships. The design of the LION cruiser was significantly improved by Vickers in co-operation with the Japanese Navy Technical Department. The new project's main armament envisaged 356 mm guns not used before and developed by Vickers. Medium gun calibre was increased from 102 mm to 152 mm. The power unit was left as on the LION class. Four ships were ordered. The first, KONGO, was built at Vickers' shipyard, the others were to be built in Japan. KIRISHIMA was built at the Mitsubishi shipyard in Yokosuka. Keel laying – 17 March 1912, launching – 1 December 1913, commissioned on 19 April 1915.

Hull

The hull was divided into six decks and twenty watertight compartments. Along the plane of symmetry, the hull was divided by a watertight bulkhead into two symmetrical parts. The engine compartment was divided into two parallel parts. Between the outer wall of the engine room and the hull there were two rows of watertight compartments. The inner one served as coal storage, while the outer was intended to protect the engine room against the effects of mine blast and torpedo explosions. 36 boilers were placed in eight rooms, four turbines in two rooms – two in each of them. Ammunition magazines were located between the engine room and boiler room.

Propulsion

The ship's propulsion was made up of four PARSONS turbines with an output of 64,000 HP and 36 YARROW boilers with an operating pressure of 19 kg/cm2 at a temperature of 270 degrees Celsius.

Armour

The broadside armour consisted of three belts on the section from turret No. 1 to turret No. 4. The first one was made of 203 mm thick plate and above it there were two 152 mm thick armour belts. From No. 1 turret to the bow stem it was 76 mm thick, from No. 4 turret to the rudder also 76 mm. Transverse bow bulkhead – 152 mm/127 mm, transverse stern bulkhead – 152 mm/203 mm. Upper deck – 38 mm. Ammunition compartments – sides 19 mm, bottom – 25 mm, top – 12.7 mm. Command post – 254 mm. Barbettes - 229 mm, casemates – 38 mm. Armour of main gun turrets - front – 254 mm, sides – 254 mm, rear – 254 mm.

Armament

Specifications	
calibre gun	356 mm
weight	86 tons
overall length	16 m
barrel length	13.74 m
thread	2.048 x 8.865 mm
volume of gun breech	294.9 cm3
rate of fire	2 rounds/minute
range	25,800 m
elevation	-5/+33 degrees
barrel life	250-280 shots
supply of ammunition	90 rounds/gun
Ammunition	
rounds of APC TYPE 5, weight 635 kg, projectile length 152.5 cm	
incendiary rounds or HE, weight 625 kg, projectile length 120 cm	
3 IS fragmentation rounds, weight 622 kg, projectile length 140 cm	

The secondary 76.2mm guns were purchased at the Elswick Arsenal and Vickers plant. Later they were built in Japan. On 25 December 1908 the designation was changed from 3"/40 Elswick Pattern Vickers Mk 2 to 3"/40-41 Year Type Model 1908. On 5 November 1917, the inch designation was changed to metric. It was eventually classified as 8 cm, although the actual calibre remained 7.62 cm. The final designation was 8 cm/40 (3 „) 41 Year Type Model 1908.

Specifications	
calibre	76.2 mm
barrel length	2.62 m
weight	600 kg
thread	1 x 5.9 mm
volume of the gun breech	2.1 cm^3
rate of fire	15 rounds/minute
range	40 degree elevation/10,740 m, 70/5,790 m
barrel life	2,700 shots
HE rounds of	5.67 kg
mount	1,253 kg
elevation	-10/+90
360 degrees manual rotation	
supply of 215 rounds per gun	

The 25 mm gun was manufactured under license from Hotchkiss. The navy made a few changes in the design, the flash absorbers on the barrels were modelled on the Rheinmetall pattern. The navy also designed their own gun mounts for them. The weapon was adopted on 6 August 1936 as 25 mm/60 (1") Type 96 (Model 1936). In total, about 33,000 of them were manufactured on one, two and three barrel mounts.

Specifications	
calibre	25mm
weight (without magazine)	115 kg
overall length	2,296 mm
barrel length	1,500 mm
thread	0.25 x 3.58 mm
barrel life	12,000 shots
theoretical rate of fire	220 rounds/minute
practical	110 rounds/minute
AT rounds	0.26 kg
HE	0.24 kg
incendiary	0.25 kg
tracer	0.25 kg
15 round magazine	
ammunition supply	2,000 rounds/gun
horizontal range	50/7,500 m
vertical range	80/5,250 m
1-barrel mount weight 185 kg	
2-barrel 1,100 kg	
3-barrel 1,800 kg	
elevation	-10/+80
horizontal rotation speed	18 degrees/sec
elevation speed	12 degrees/sec

Modifications

1921 - 356 mm gun elevation increased from 25 to 33 degrees thus increasing range from 25,800 m to 29,000 m.

1927-30 - armour thickness above the engine room increased to 80 mm and above the ammunition compartments to 120 mm. Anti-torpedo chambers - so-called „bulges" - were added, which increased the hull width by more than 1 metre. Underwater torpedo tubes were removed. The fore superstructure was raised, expanding it around the front mast taking the characteristic "pagoda" shape of Japanese battleships. The 36 Yarrow boilers were exchanged for 6 Ro Go boilers of a larger version for mixed fuel (25kg/cm2 at 320 degrees) and 4 Ro Go boilers of the small version fired with oil fuel. The fore funnel and bow boiler room were dismantled. An E1Y seaplane launched by a crane was taken on board. On 30 May 1931, the ship was reclassified from a battlecruiser to a battleship.

1932-33 - anti-aircraft protection strengthened. 76 mm guns removed, instead 4 twin-barrel 127 mm guns and 4 x 40mm guns were installed. A seaplane catapult was added. 2-3 E4N2 seaplanes were carried from then on.

1931-36 - modernization of the power unit with an output of 136,000 HP. The four main turbines were exchanged for Kanpon type. Boilers were fired with oil fuel and increased to 8 units. The stern was extended by 7.6 m to increase the speed to 30.5 knots. 356 mm gun elevation angle increased to 43 degrees, range now 33,000 m. The 152 mm gun elevation angle was also increased from 15 to 30 degrees, their number reduced to 14. 40 mm guns and 13.2 mm machine guns were abandoned as inefficient. Instead, 10 x 25mm 2-barrel mounts were installed. Torpedo tubes were removed. The superstructure was expanded. The seaplanes were replaced with 2 x type E8N1 (DAVE) and 1 x type E7K1 (ALF)

1939 - armour of turrets and barbettes strengthened.

1940 - E13A (JAKE) and F1M (PETE) seaplanes were introduced.

Port side view.

Specifications		
	1915	1940
Standard displacement	26,330 tons	31,980 tons
Full displacement	–	38,200 tons
Overall length	214.58 m	222.20 m
Beam	28.04 m	31.09 m
Draf	8.22 m	9.60 m
Propulsion	4x Parsons turbines 4 x Kanpon turbines	36 x Yarrow boilers 8 x Kanpon boilers
Output	64,000 HP	136,000 HP
Speed	27.5 kn	30.5 kn
Range	9,500 nm/14	10,000 nm/18
Fuel supply	4,200 t of coal, 1,100 t of fuel oil	6,330 t of fuel oil
Armament	8 x 356 mm/2	8 x 356 mm/2
	16 x 152 mm	14 x 152 mm
	8 x 76 mm	8 x 127mm/2
	8 x 533 mm tubes	–
	10 x 25 mm/2	
Aviation equipment Kure Type 2 Mod 5 catapult	2 x JAKE E13A seaplanes	1 x PETE F1M seaplane
Crew	1,221	1,393

Operational history

The keel was laid at Mitsubishi Zosen Kaisha's Shipyard in Nagasaki on 17 March 1912. On 1 December 1913, the ship was launched. It was named KIRISHIMA („ISLAND OF MIST" - the name of the mountain on the island of Kyushu in Kagoshima Prefecture). On 19 April 1915 the ship was commissioned, her first skipper was Commander Kamaya. On 12 June 1915, along with HARUNA, KIRISHIMA was assigned to the 1st Battleship Squadron, then transferred to the 3rd Battleship Squadron. The squadron was stationed in Sasebo, the main base of the Sasebo Maritime District. During World War One, the ship operated in China from 1916, without participating in combat operations. In July 1918 she travelled to Canada with Prince Arthur of Connaught aboard. In the interwar years she operated off the coast of China. There were frequent changes of commanders during this period. In September 1923 she helped victims of a major earthquake that ruined Tokyo and Yokohama.

On 1 September 1924 the battleship was transferred to the 4th Battleship Squadron of the 2nd Fleet. From 1 December 1926, the ship was in reserve.

From May 1927 to April 1930, the ship was modernized and renovated.

On 1 December 1930 KIRISHIMA was assigned to the 1st Battleship Squadron of the 1st Fleet.

From April to December 1932, she operated in Chinese waters in connection with the so-called Shanghai Incident.

In December 1932, the battleship was withdrawn into reserve and until spring 1933 modernization of the AA weapons was carried out.

In the period from 18 November 1934 to 8 June 1936, KIRISHIMA underwent a major rebuild and modernization at the shipyard in Sasebo. After returning to service, along with other KONGO-type ships, she was assigned to the 3rd Battleship Squadron. In 1937, during the Second Sino-Japanese War, together with the battleship HARUNA, she carried 1st Battalion of the 68th Infantry Regiment and two battalions from the 3rd Infantry Division to the area of operations. Her seaplanes carried out two raids on Shanghai. The battleship stayed on and off in Chinese waters until 1939.

From November 1939, modernization - strengthening of the armor on turrets and barbettes - was carried out at the shipyard in Sasebo.

After Japan entered WW2, the battleship KIRISHIMA participated in all the important operations of the Japanese fleet, mainly as an escort for aircraft carriers. She participated in operations together with the battleship HIEI, with whom she formed a pair within a squadron. From November to the end of December 1941, the pair was the cover for aircraft carriers of the 1st Fleet, among others during the attack on Pearl Harbor. At the end of December (27-30), she underwent a short renovation at the shipyard in Kure during which wave damage was repaired.

On 14 January 1942, both battleships were transferred to Truk, from where they escorted aircraft carriers supporting the capture of Rabaul and Kavieng.

On 19 February, they escorted aircraft carriers attacking Darwin Harbour. At the end of February, they protected aircraft carriers in the Java Sea, attacking targets in Java.

On 1 March 1942, together with HIEI, unsuccessfully shelled the American destroyer USS EDSALL. KIRISHIMA fired 87 356 mm shells and 62 152mm shells. Eventually, the destroyer was sunk with the help of aircraft.

From 26 March to 10 April, along with the entire squadron, she protected aircraft carriers during a raid into the Indian Ocean. During the attack on the British base in Colombo, the destroyer HMS TENEDOS, auxiliary cruiser HMS HECTOR and Norwegian tanker SOLL were sunk and the transports BENLEDI and CLAN MURDOCH and tender LUCIA were damaged. 26 aircraft were destroyed at the airfield. In the afternoon, the British cruisers DORSETSHIRE and CORNWALL were sunk. In total, 29 ships were sunk during the raid.

During the Battle of Midway, KIRISHIMA and HARUNA, as part of a support group, helped to fend off American aviation attacks by barrage fire from their main guns. KIRISHIMA was attacked by the submarine NAUTILUS. She fired a torpedo, which missed its target. At the end of the battle, she assisted the burning aircraft carrier HIRYU. After her sinking, she took aboard survivors from sunken aircraft carriers who had been rescued by destroyers.

On 14 July HIEI and KIRISHIMA were assigned to the 11th Battleship Squadron of the 3rd Fleet operating in the area of the SOLOMON Islands.

Top view.

On 24 August they protected aircraft carriers during the battle near the eastern SOLOMONS.

At night on 14 October, she shielded the battleships KONGO and HARUNA during the bombardment of the airfield at Guadalcanal. During the next night, she was covering the force of cruisers repeating the action.

On 25-26 October she protected a group of aircraft carriers at the Battle of Santa Cruz. During the battle on 25 October she was attacked by B-17 bombers but unsuccessfully. Seaplanes from the battleship damaged an American CATALINA flying boat.

On 26 October KIRISHIMA was attacked by three dive bombers - unsuccessfully.

On 10 November KIRISHIMA and HIEI set sail from THE SHORTLAND ANCHORAGE with the mission of bombarding the airfield at Guadalcanal in connection with the operation of delivering munitions to the island. As a result, the first battle of Guadalcanal took place.

On the night of 12/13 November during a short-range fight KIRISHIMA damaged the two American cruisers SAN FRANCISCO and HELENA and two destroyers by firing 57 356 mm shells and 313 152 mm shells. She was hit by a 203 mm shell from SAN FRANCISCO. After the battle, she tried to tow the damaged battleship HIEI but without success. HIEI was scuttled by her own crew.

On the night of 14 November, a landing operation was planned to provide troops and supplies for Guadalcanal.

On the night of 13/14, the force of heavy cruisers CHOKAI, KINUGASA, MAYA, SUZUYA bombarded the airfield destroying one B-17 bomber and 17 fighters. 32 other planes were damaged. However, during the day, the superiority of American air power allowed it to attack the returning force, sinking the cruiser KINUGASA. A Japanese convoy was also detected, six transports perished and one was forced to retreat. In the evening 4 surviving transports and 11 destroyers closed on the island. Convoy commander Rear Admiral Tanaka, fearing bombing during unloading, ordered the ships to be run aground. 2,000 soldiers with light weapons and some supplies were disembarked. However, during the day the ships were destroyed by aircraft along with the rest of the supplies. The landing cover was composed of the battleship KIRISHIMA, two heavy cruisers ATAGO and TAKAO, two light cruisers NAGARA and SENDAI and nine destroyers under the command of Vice Admiral Kondo.

The American TF64 that was sent to prevent the landing consisted of the battleships WASHINGTON and SOUTH DAKOTA and 4 destroyers commanded by Rear Admiral Lee. The American force sailing to the shores of Guadalcanal was spotted by a reconnaissance group (SENDAI, SHIKINAMI). The ships were reported as cruisers. The cruiser NAGARA and six destroyers which were to sail around the island of Savo from the west and intercept the Americans were detached from the main force.

At 2252 hrs the American force made a turn now along the coast of Guadalcanal. Upon turning, the cruiser SENDAI and the destroyer SHIKINAMI were sighted behind it.

Around 2317 hrs the battleships opened fire at them from 10 km using radar detection. The Japanese ships turned and managed to escape.

Around 2330 hrs, four American destroyers leading TF64 were destroyed by Japanese ships.

The battleship SOUTH DAKOTA was drawn into a lonely fight with Rear Admiral Kondo's team. She was severely damaged.

The battleship WASHINGTON escaped detection and surprised Japanese ships at a distance of 7,500 metres.

Exactly at midnight, first firing illuminating flares and then firing all her guns, WASHINGTON focused on the battleship KIRISHIMA.

Already WASHINGTON's first salvo reached its target and the ship's rudder gear was damaged. Next 16-inch and 5-inch gunfire led to the complete demolition of the battleship. WASHINGTON fired 75 16-inch shells hitting directly 9 times and 40 times with 5-inch shells.

The whole engagement between KIRISHIMA and WASHINGTON lasted only 7 minutes.

KIRISHIMA sank at 0320 hrs near her sister ship HIEI.

The Japanese Battleship *Kirishima* 1940.

The Japanese Battleship *Kirishima* 1940.

Bow view.

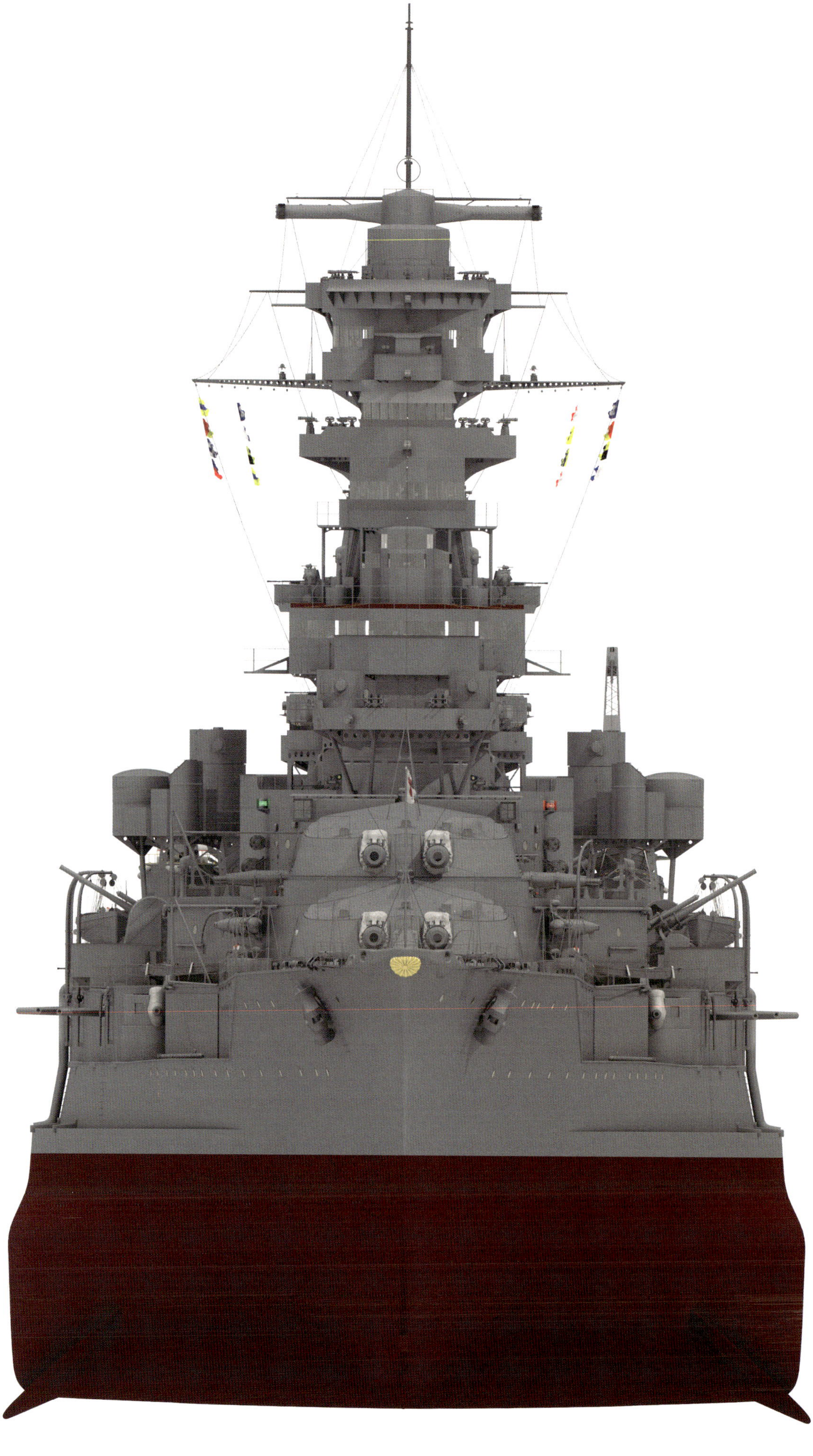

Stern view.

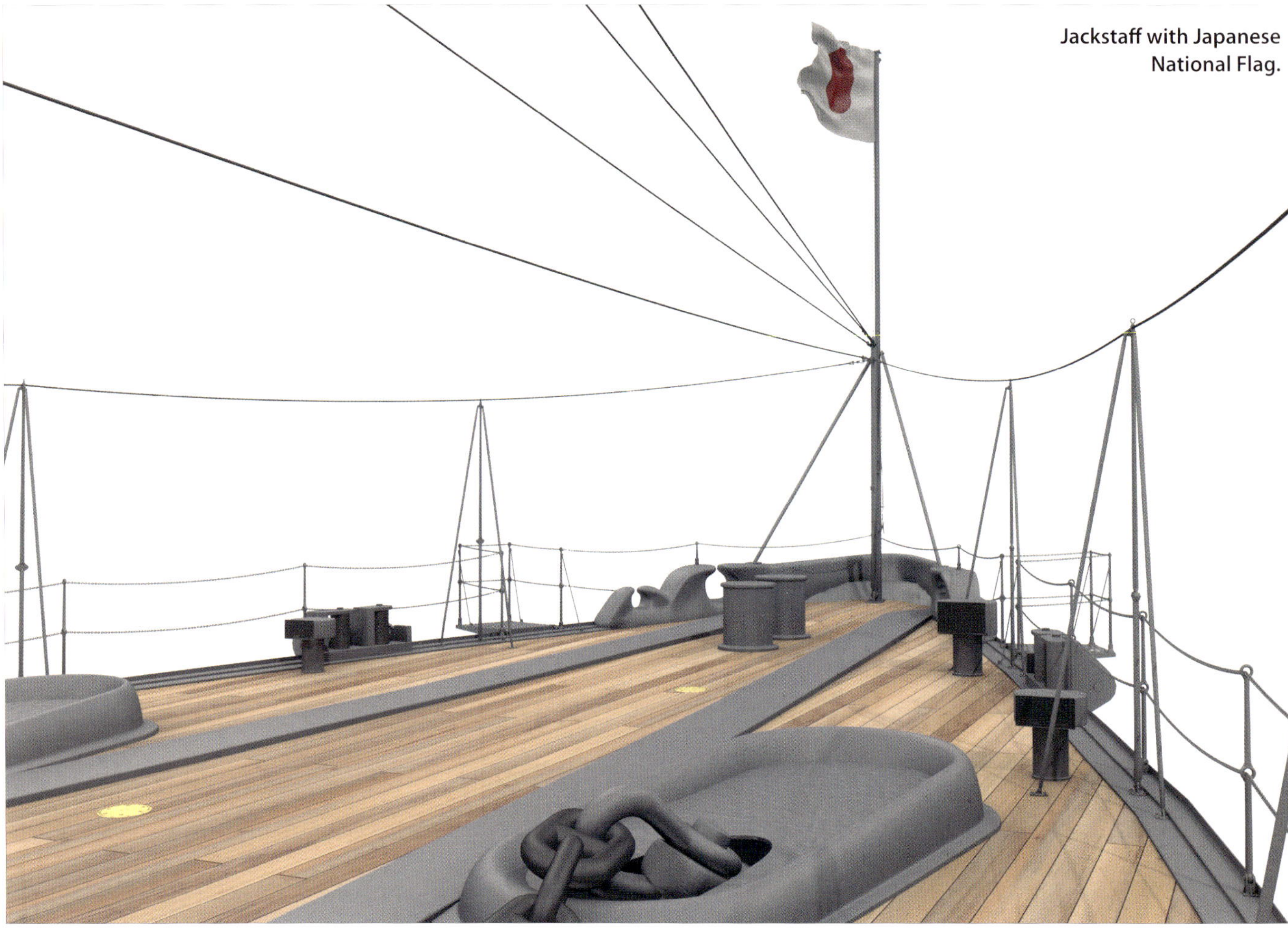
Jackstaff with Japanese National Flag.

Bow anchor.

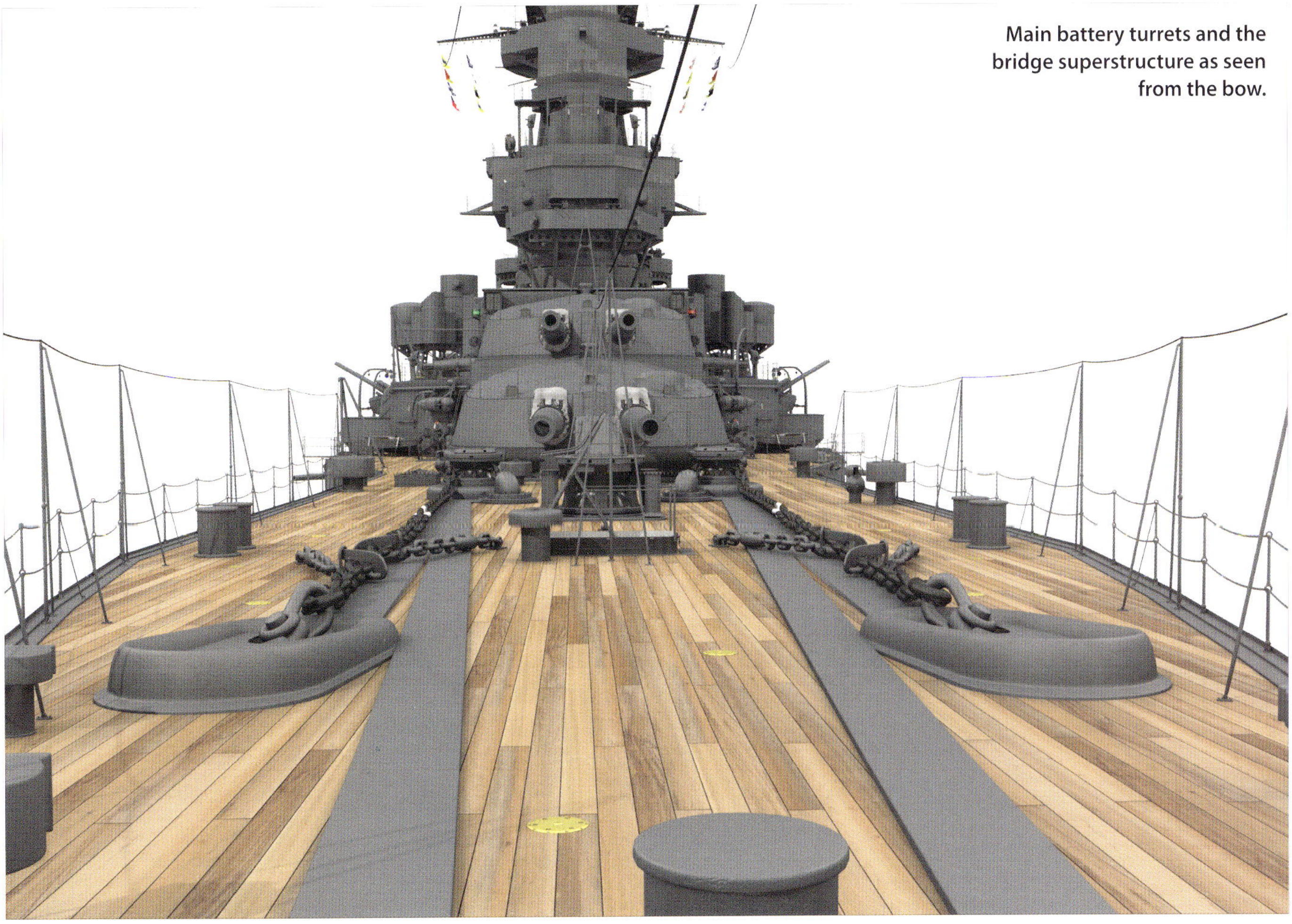

Main battery turrets and the bridge superstructure as seen from the bow.

Auxiliary capstan as seen from the starboard bow.

Bridge superstructure as seen from the foredeck.

Starboard side main anchor capstan.

Lower foredeck with a boom for handling ship boats in a stowed position.

Boom for handling ship boats on the lower deck starboard side shown in the stowed position.

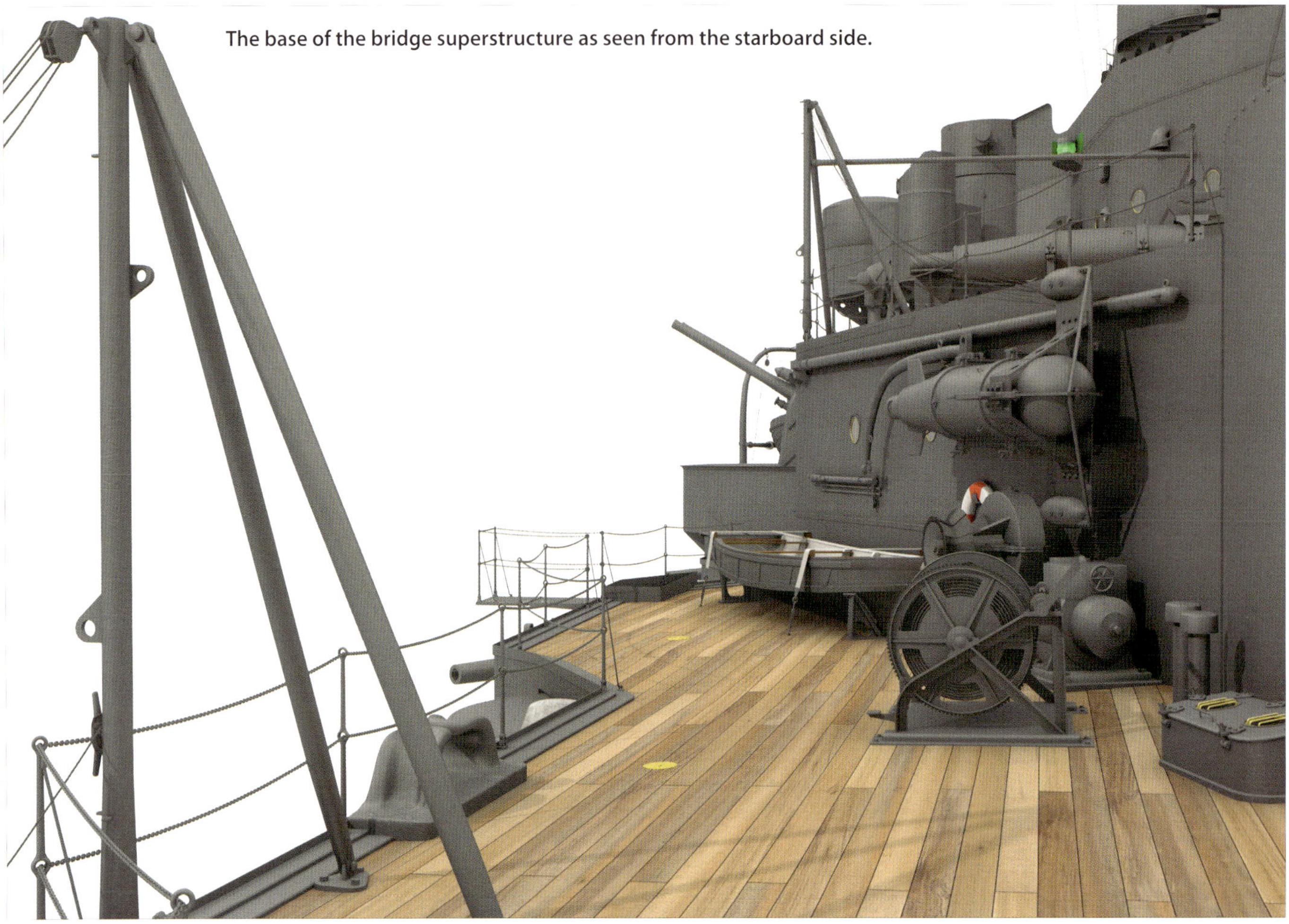

The base of the bridge superstructure as seen from the starboard side.

Foredeck hatch behind the main battery gun turret No. 1.

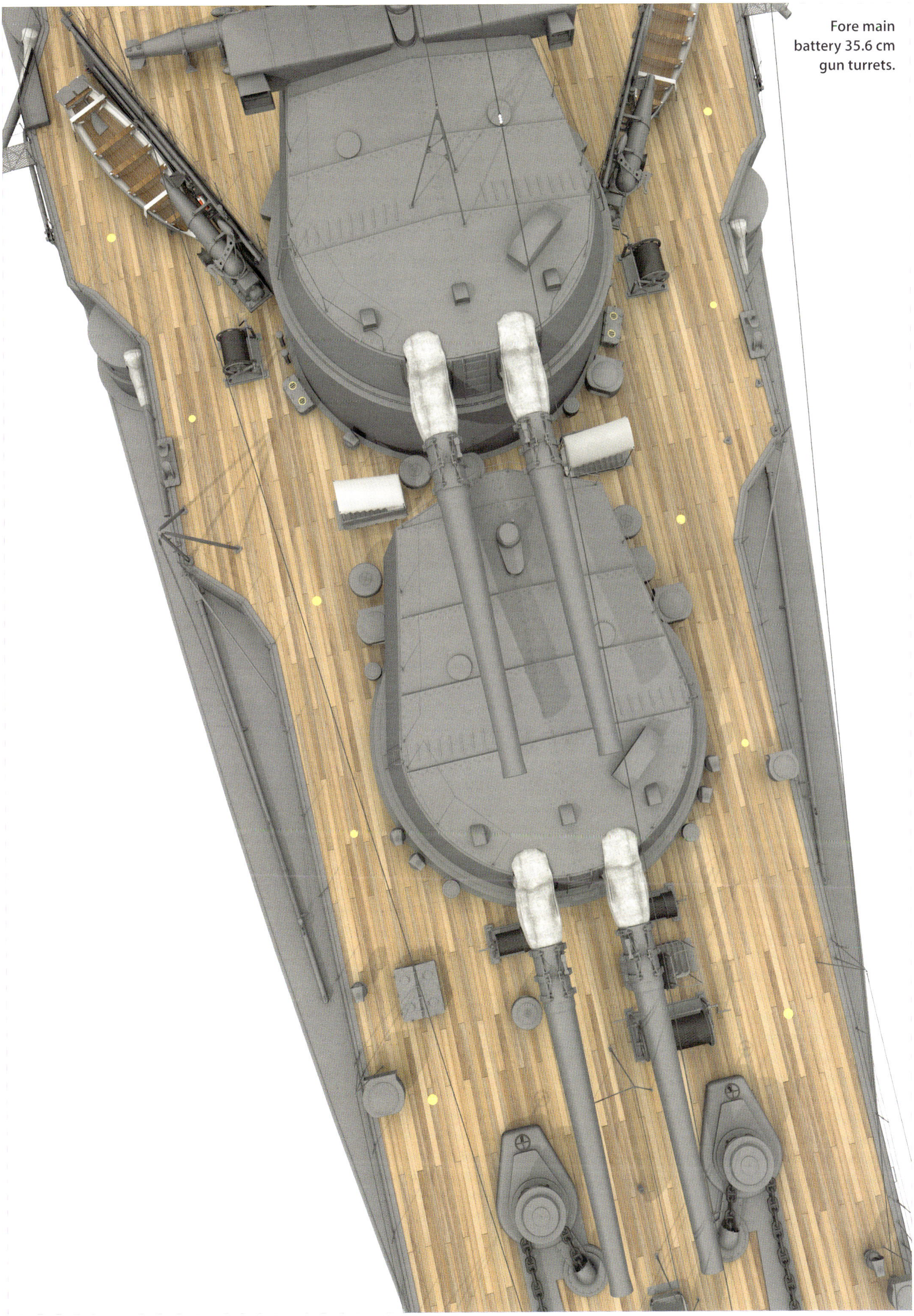

Fore main battery 35.6 cm gun turrets.

Bridge superstructure.

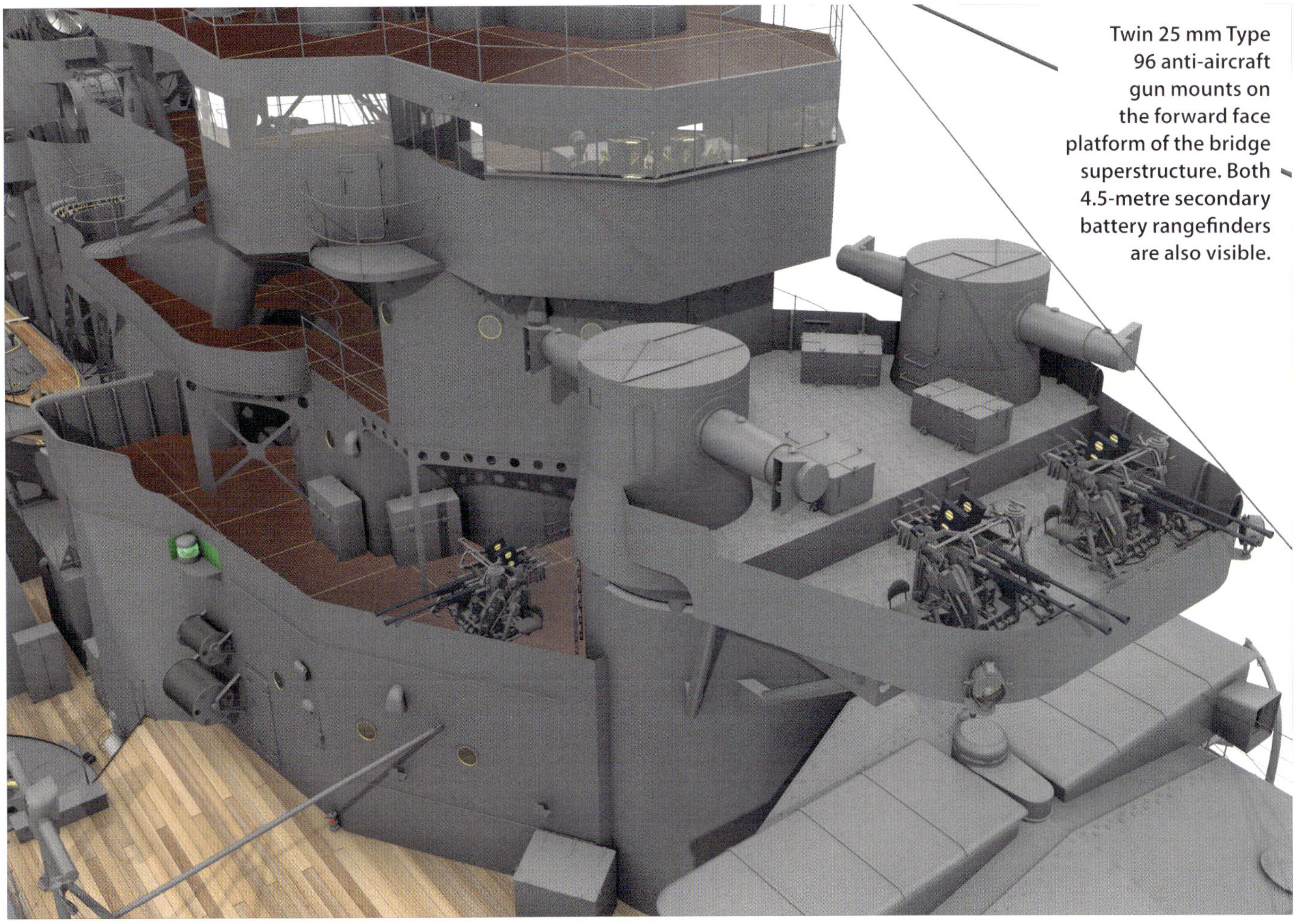

Twin 25 mm Type 96 anti-aircraft gun mounts on the forward face platform of the bridge superstructure. Both 4.5-metre secondary battery rangefinders are also visible.

Main battery 35.6 cm gun turret No. 2.

Starboard side secondary battery 15.2 cm guns in casemates.

Base of the bridge superstructure as seen from the starboard side.

Paravane stored on the deck on the starboard side of the bridge superstructure.

The bride superstructure as seen from starboard side.

The bow section as seen from the position of the 12.7 cm Type 89 gun mount at the base of the bridge superstructure.

Bridge superstructure platform braces.

A twin 25 mm Type 96 anti-aircraft gun mounted on the starboard side of the first deck of the bridge superstructure.

Admiral's deck.

Twin 25mm Type 96 anti-aircraft gun mount on the bridge tower.

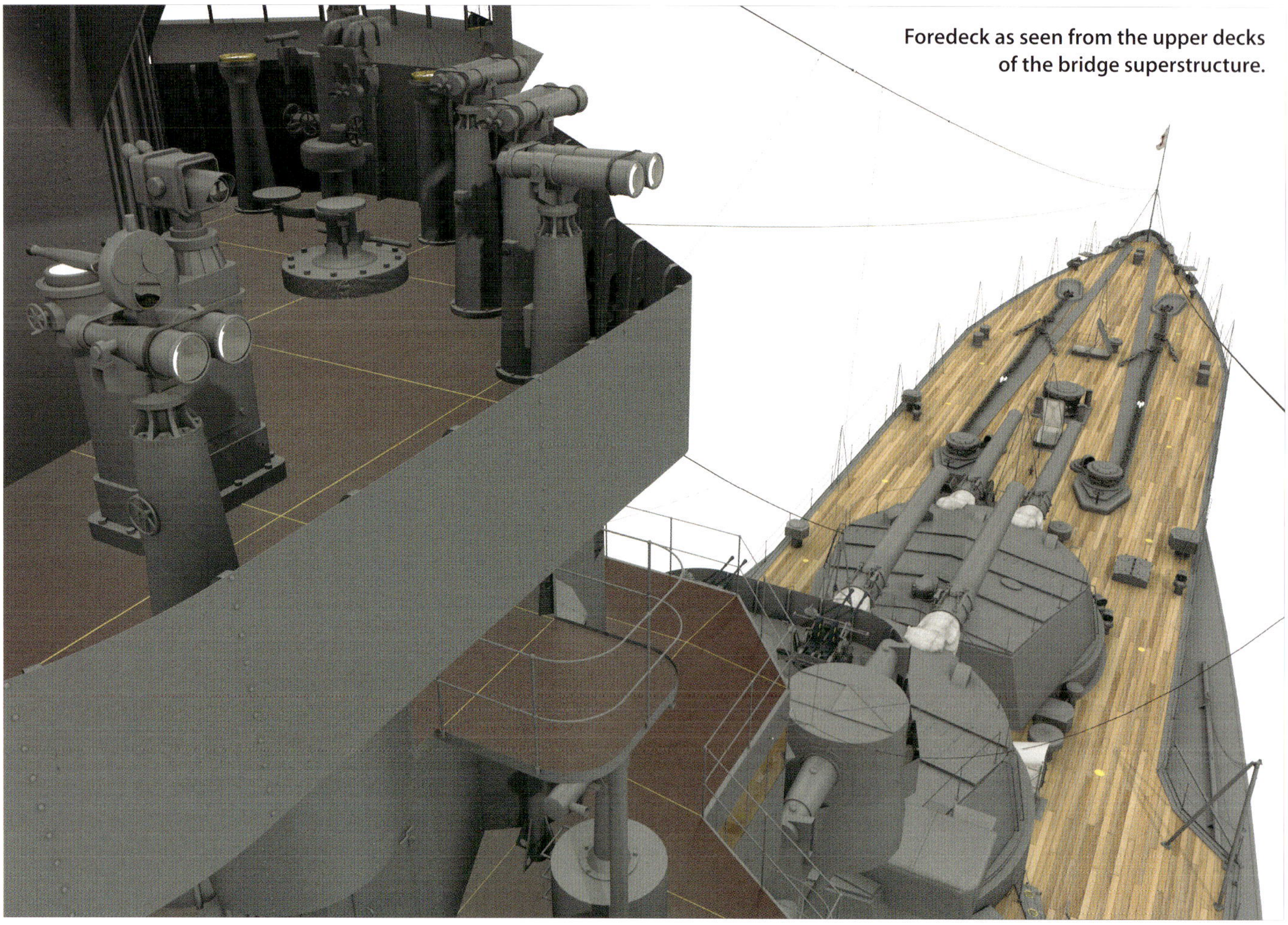

Foredeck as seen from the upper decks of the bridge superstructure.

Top of the bridge superstructure with the 10-metre rangefinder and observation posts.

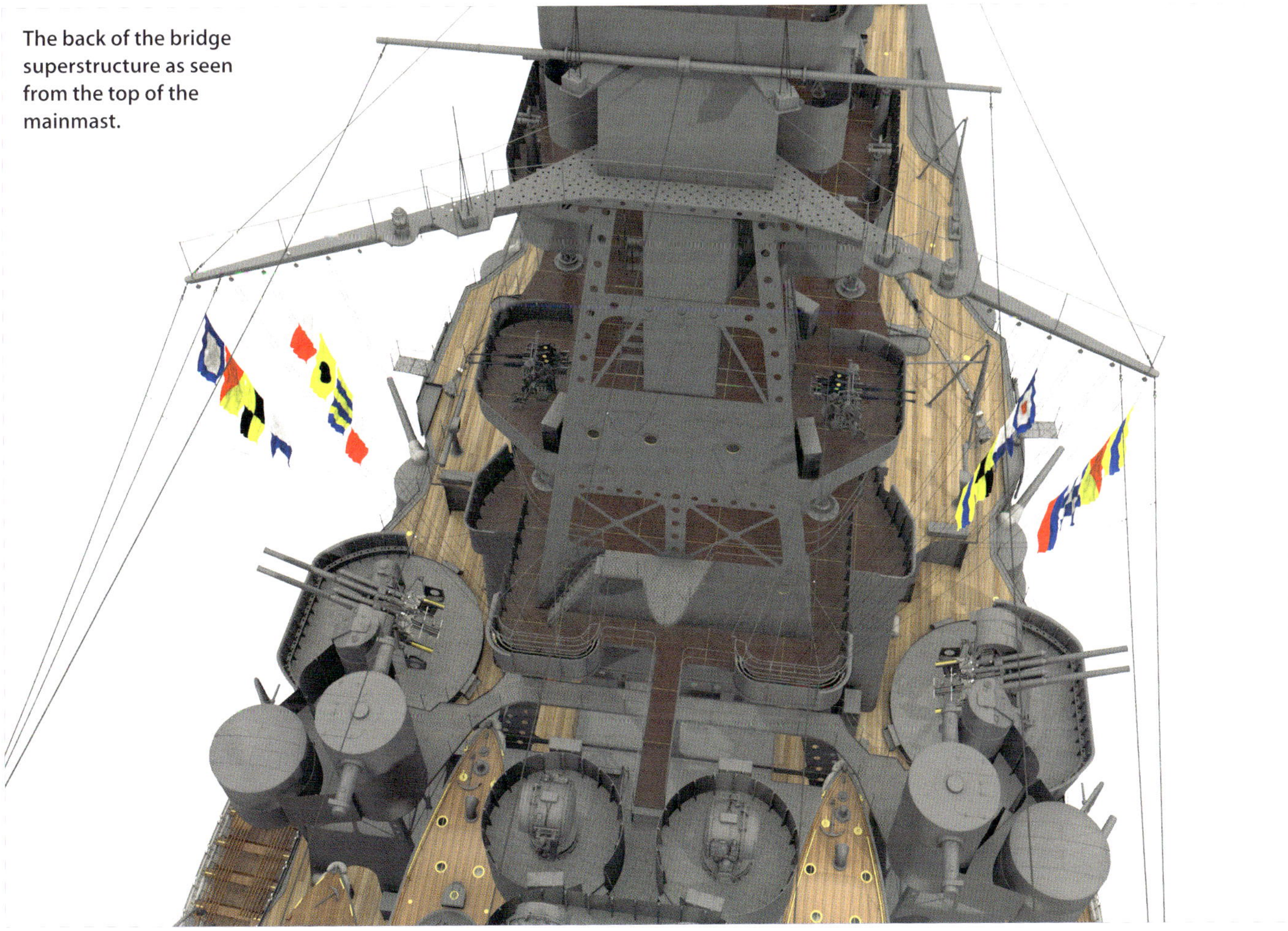

The back of the bridge superstructure as seen from the top of the mainmast.

The back side of the upper platforms of the bridge superstructure.

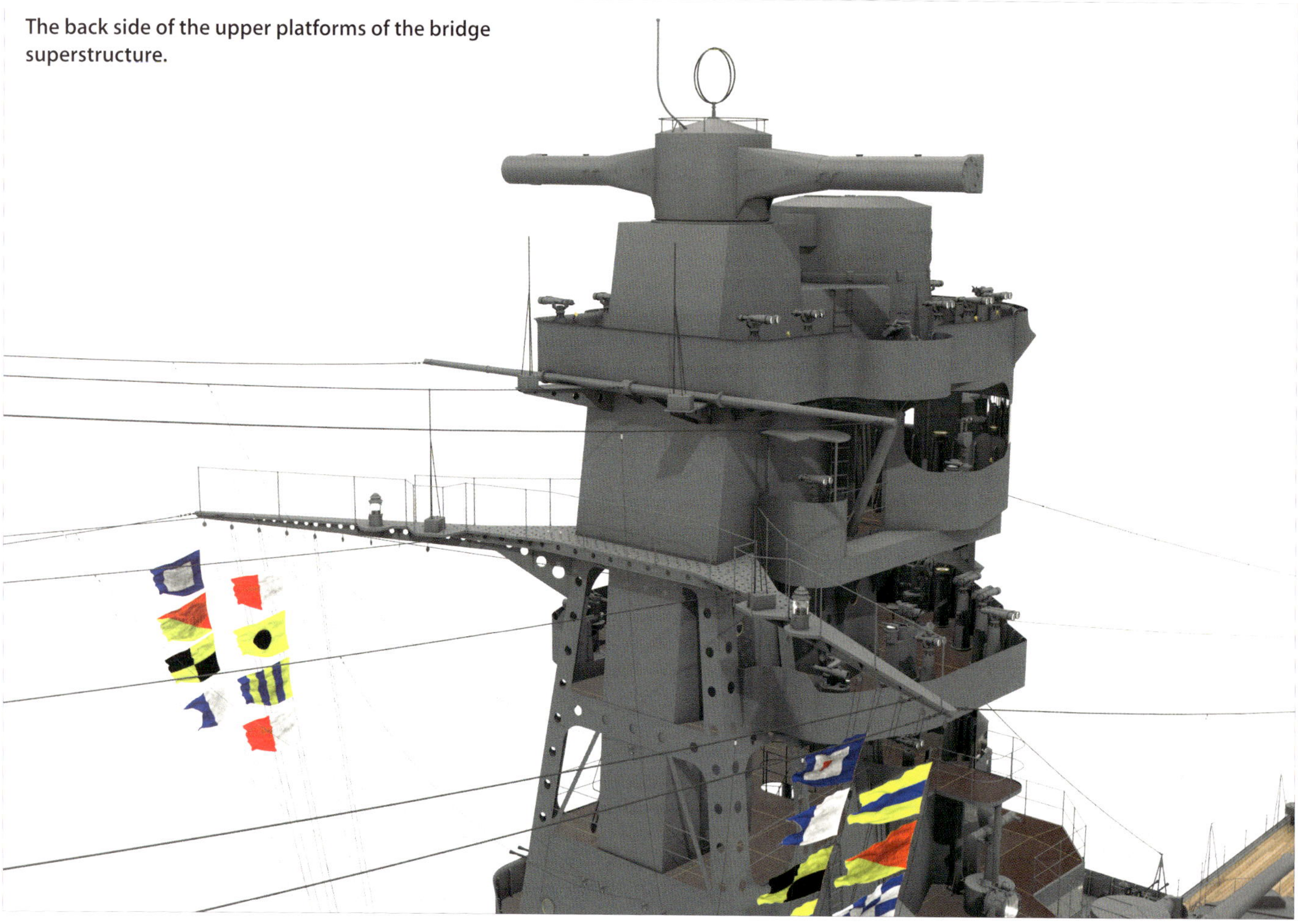

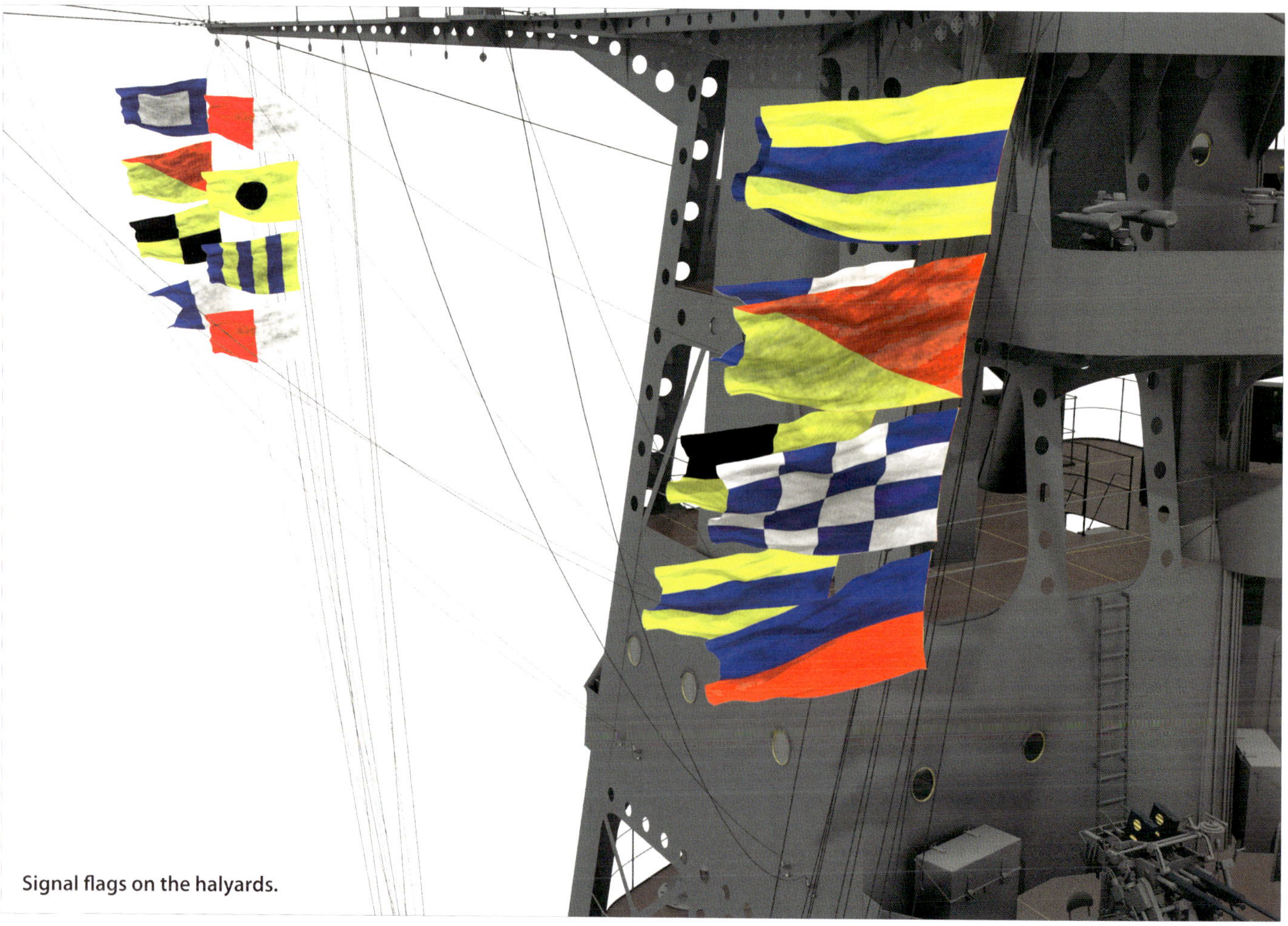

Signal flags on the halyards.

The bridge superstructure as seen from the starboard side. The reinforcements of its decks are visible.

4.5-metre secondary battery rangefinder and the observation posts on the starboard side.

The midship observation and 4.5-metre rangefinder posts as seen from the starboard side deck.

Midship section as seen from the port side.

A 12.7 cm Type 89 gun at the base of the bridge superstructure.

12.7 cm Type 89 gun mount on the starboard side of the bridge superstructure.

Starboard side view of the bow section.

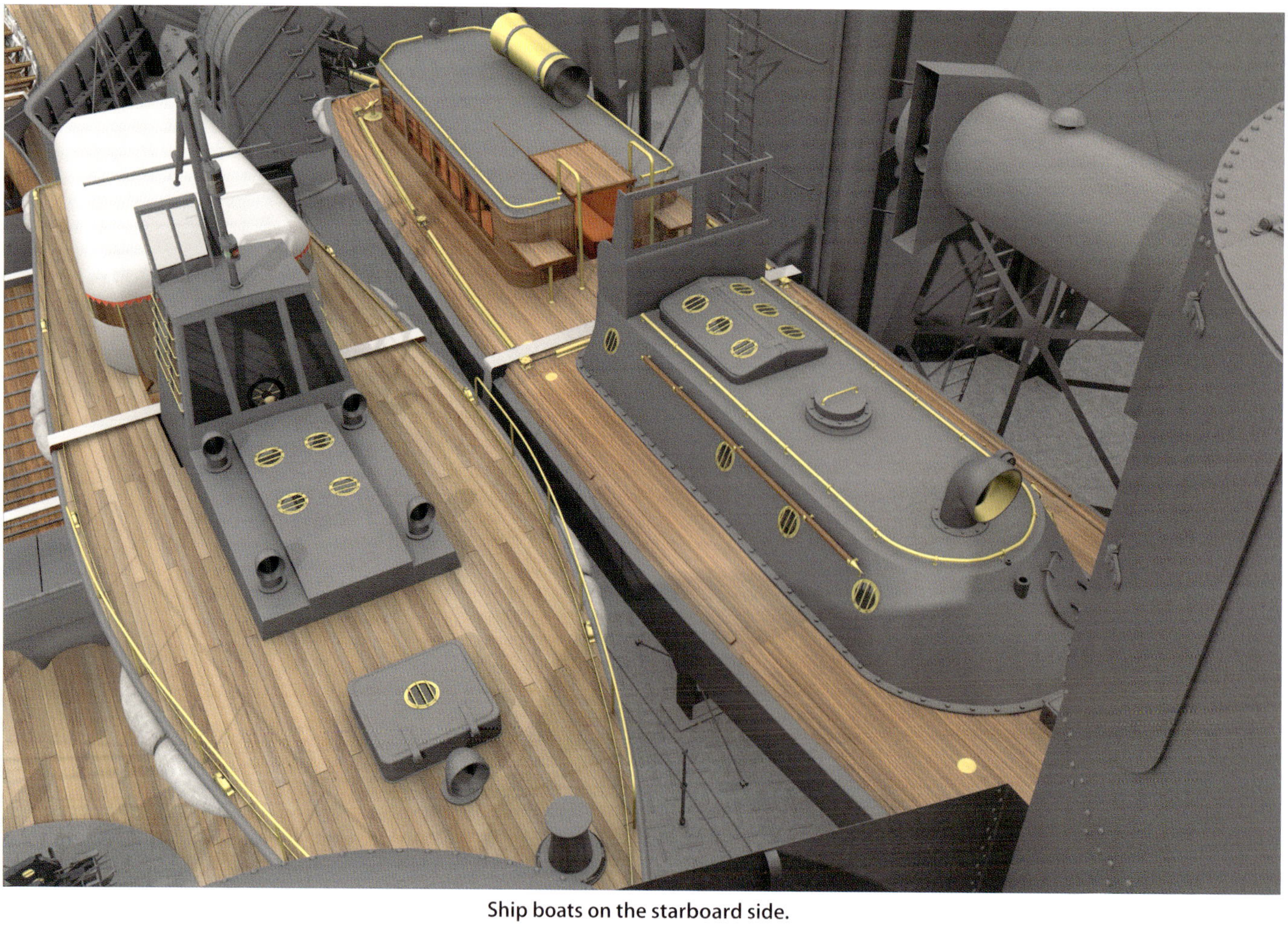

Ship boats on the starboard side.

110 cm searchlight platforms around the funnel.

Admiral's deck as seen from the first funnel.

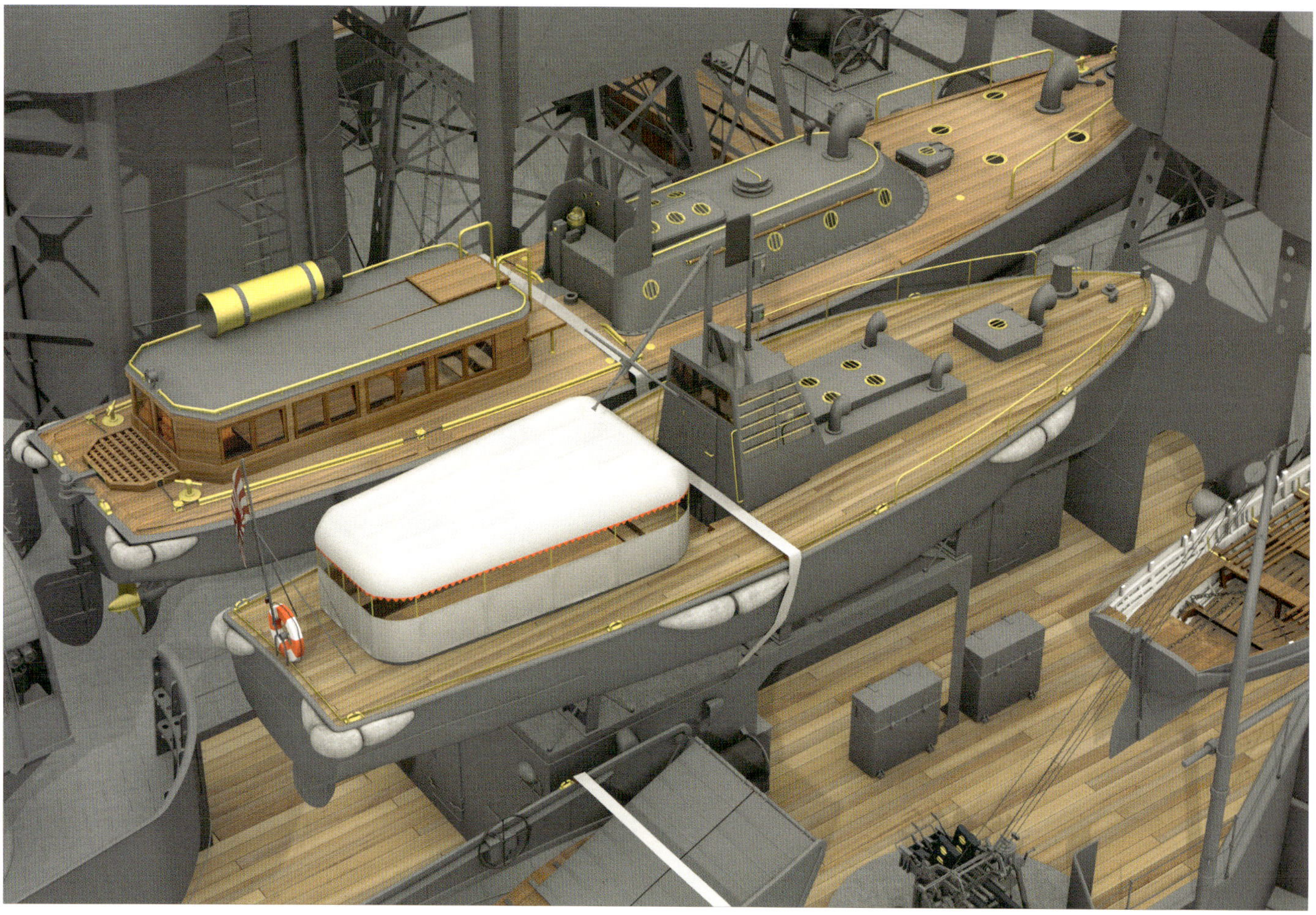
17-metre motor pinnace – ceremonial barge and a 12-metre motor boat on the superstructure abreast the funnel.

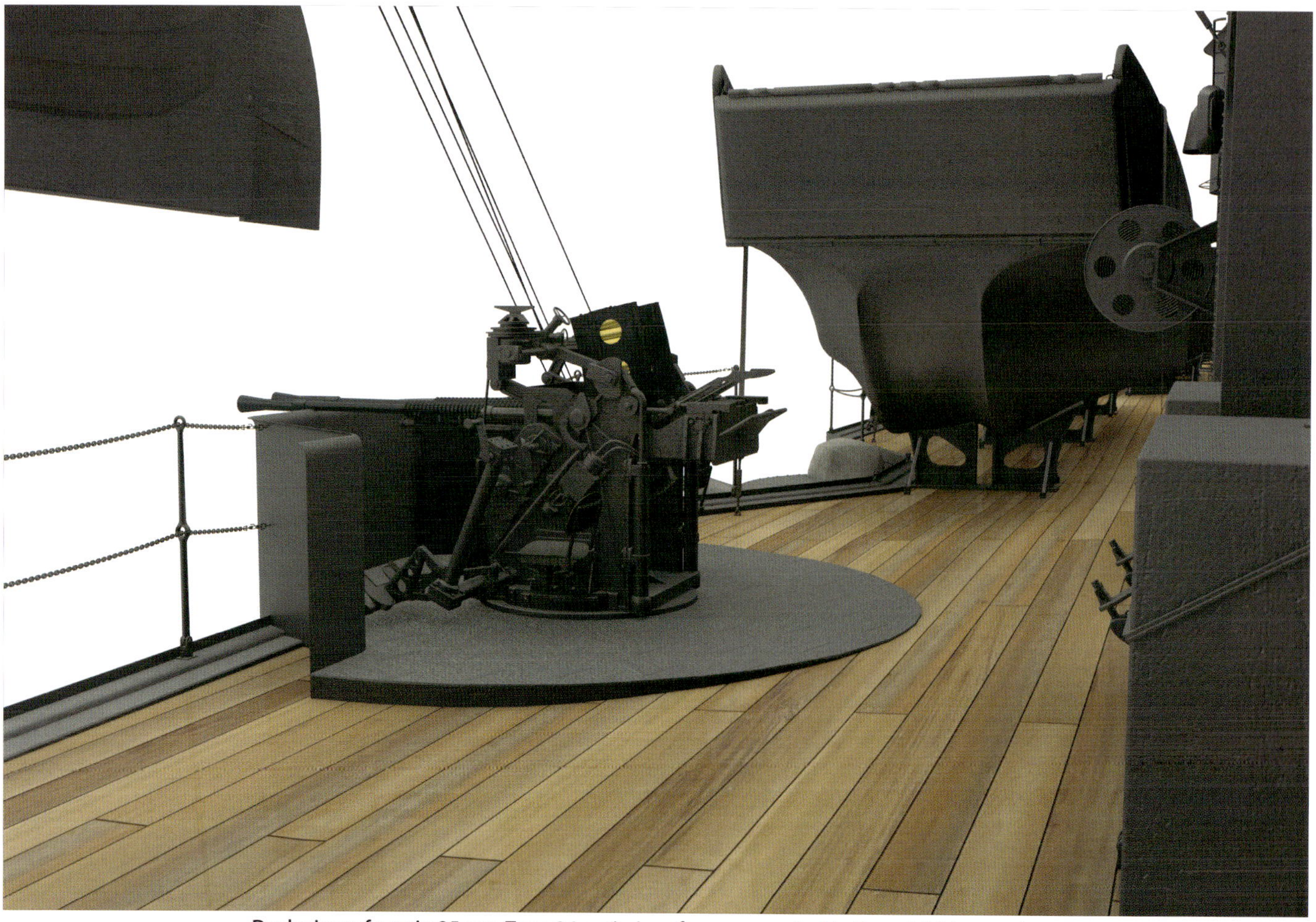
Deck view of a twin 25 mm Type 96 anti-aircraft gun mounted in the midships section.

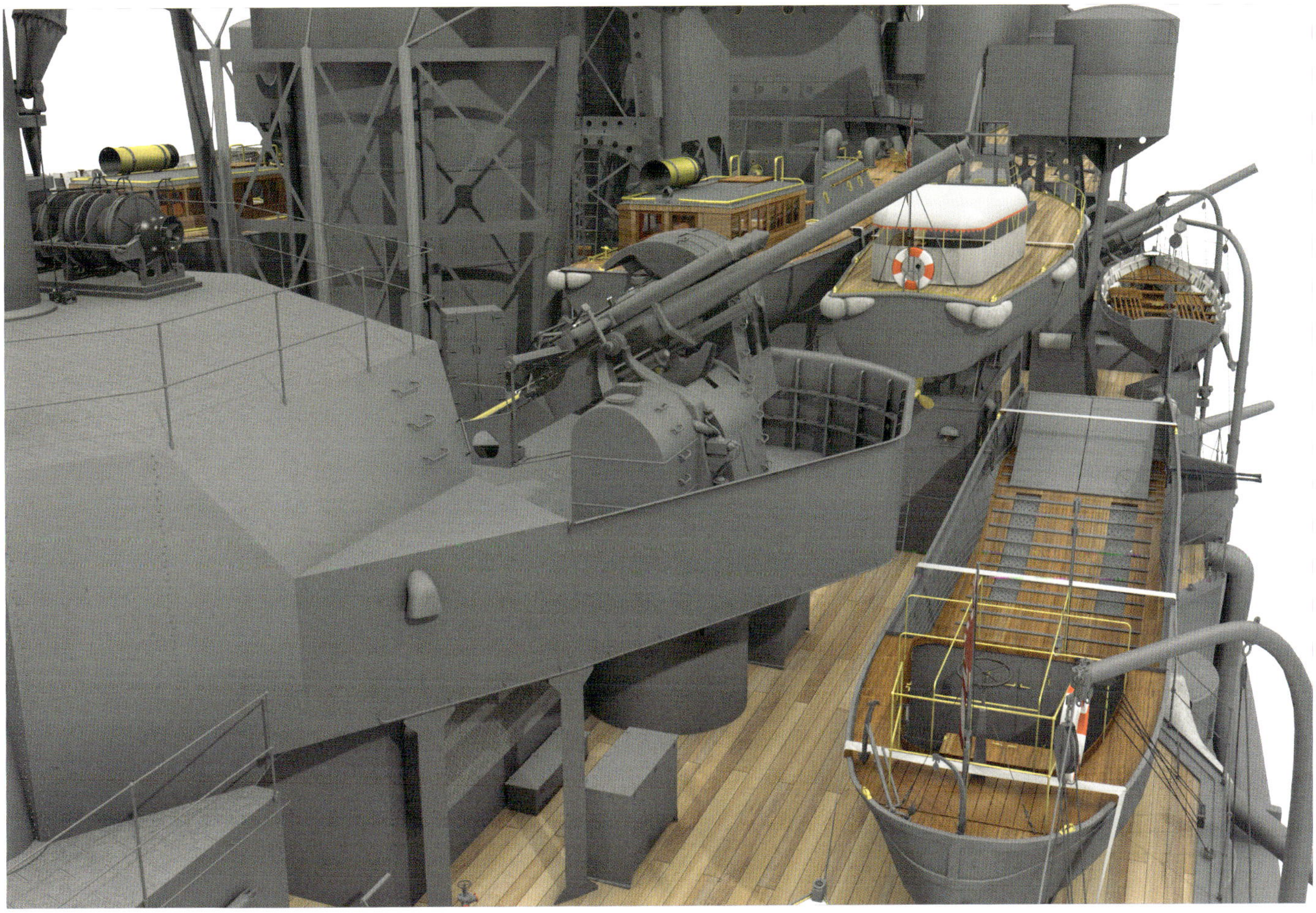

Starboard side midship section with 12.7 cm Type 89 guns in vicinity of the mainmast.

Midship section as seen from the starboard side. An 11-metre landing boat stowed on the rails is visible.

12.7 cm Type 89 gun mount in vicinity of the mainmast.

The deck below the mainmast.

Twin 25 mm Type 96 anti-aircraft gun mount located between the legs of the mainmast.

Mainmast with the crane for handling ship boats.

Aft superstructure observation posts.

Aft superstructure.

The top of the aft superstructure with 4.5-metre rangefinder and observation posts.

Starboard side view at the superstructure at the base of the mainmast.

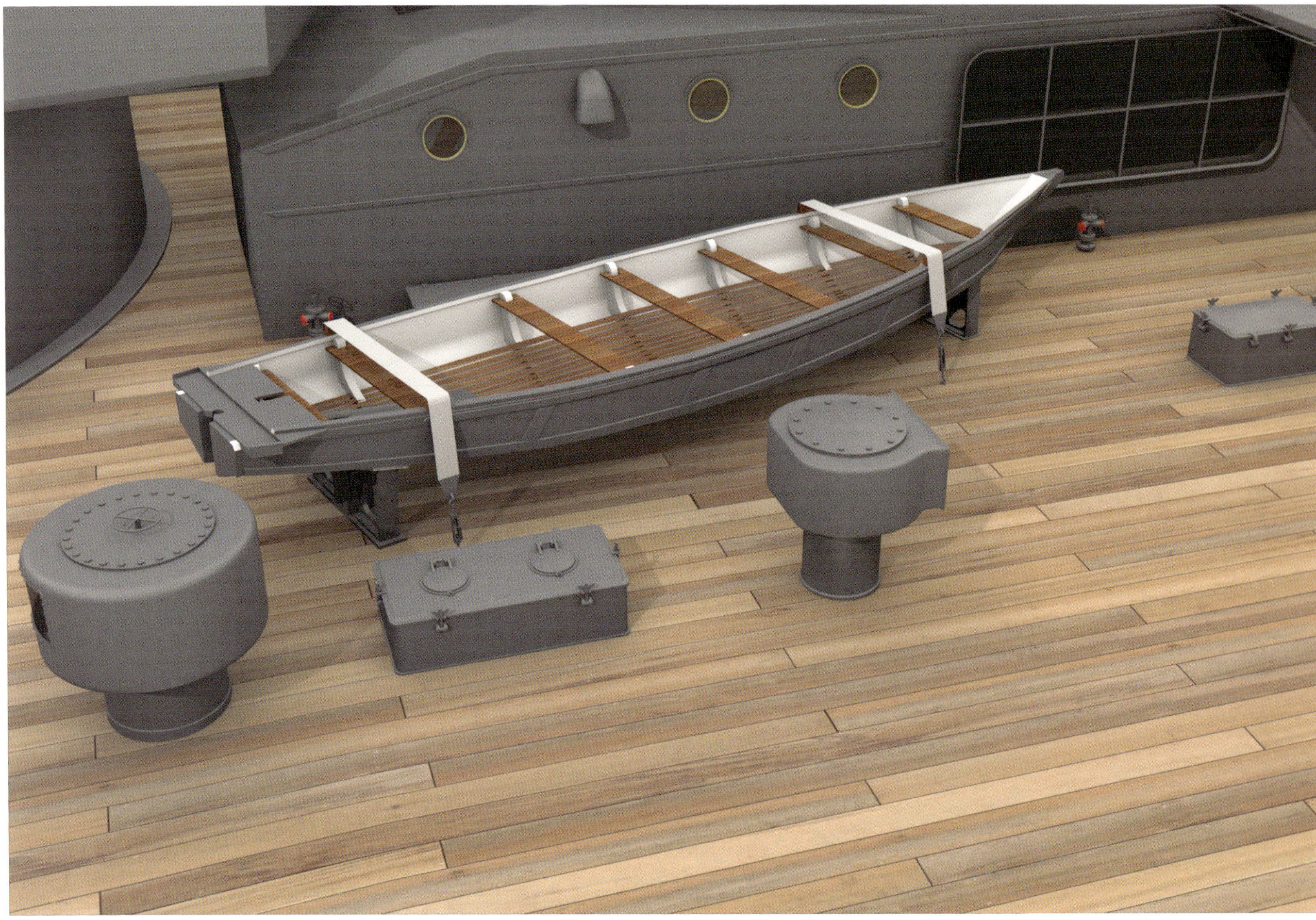

Deck fittings at the base of the aft superstructure.

Aft superstructure and the second funnel as seen from the starboard side.

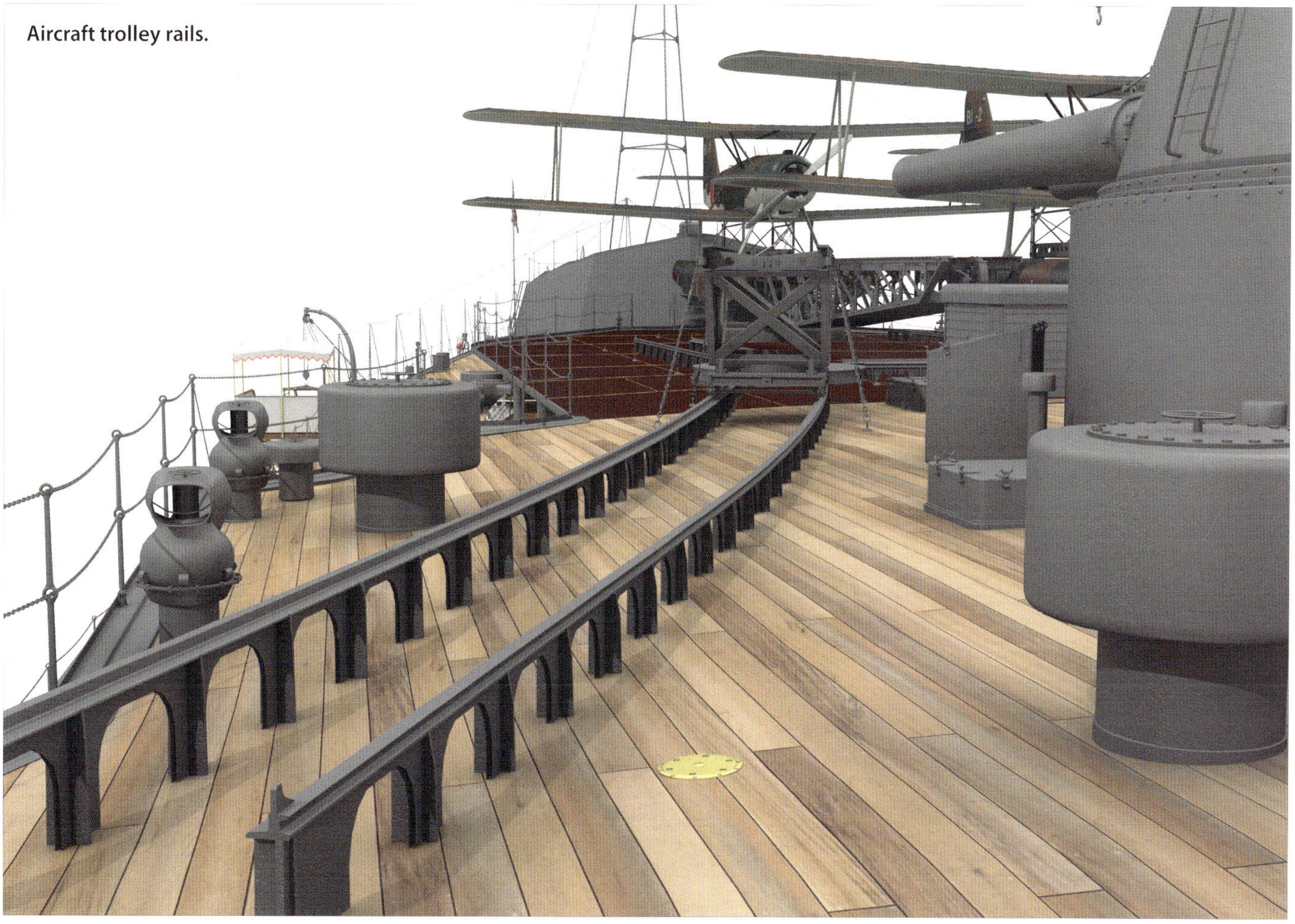
Aircraft trolley rails.

Quarterdeck as seen from the main battery turret No.3.

Floatplane trolley.

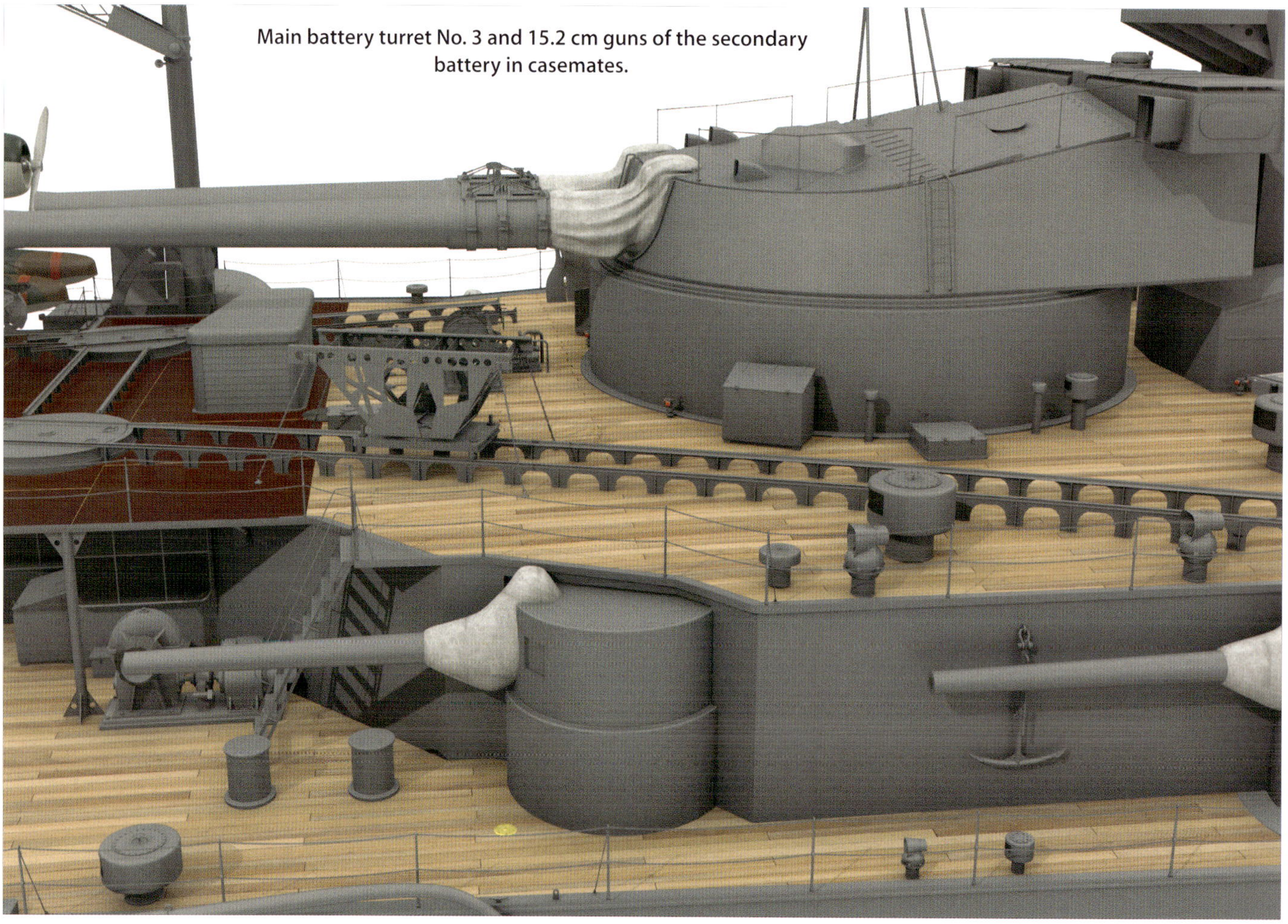

Main battery turret No. 3 and 15.2 cm guns of the secondary battery in casemates.

Aft superstructure with main battery 35.6 cm gun turret No. 3.

Aft deck below the aircraft deck. Its various fittings are visible.

Kawanishi E7K2 "Alf" floatplane on the catapult.

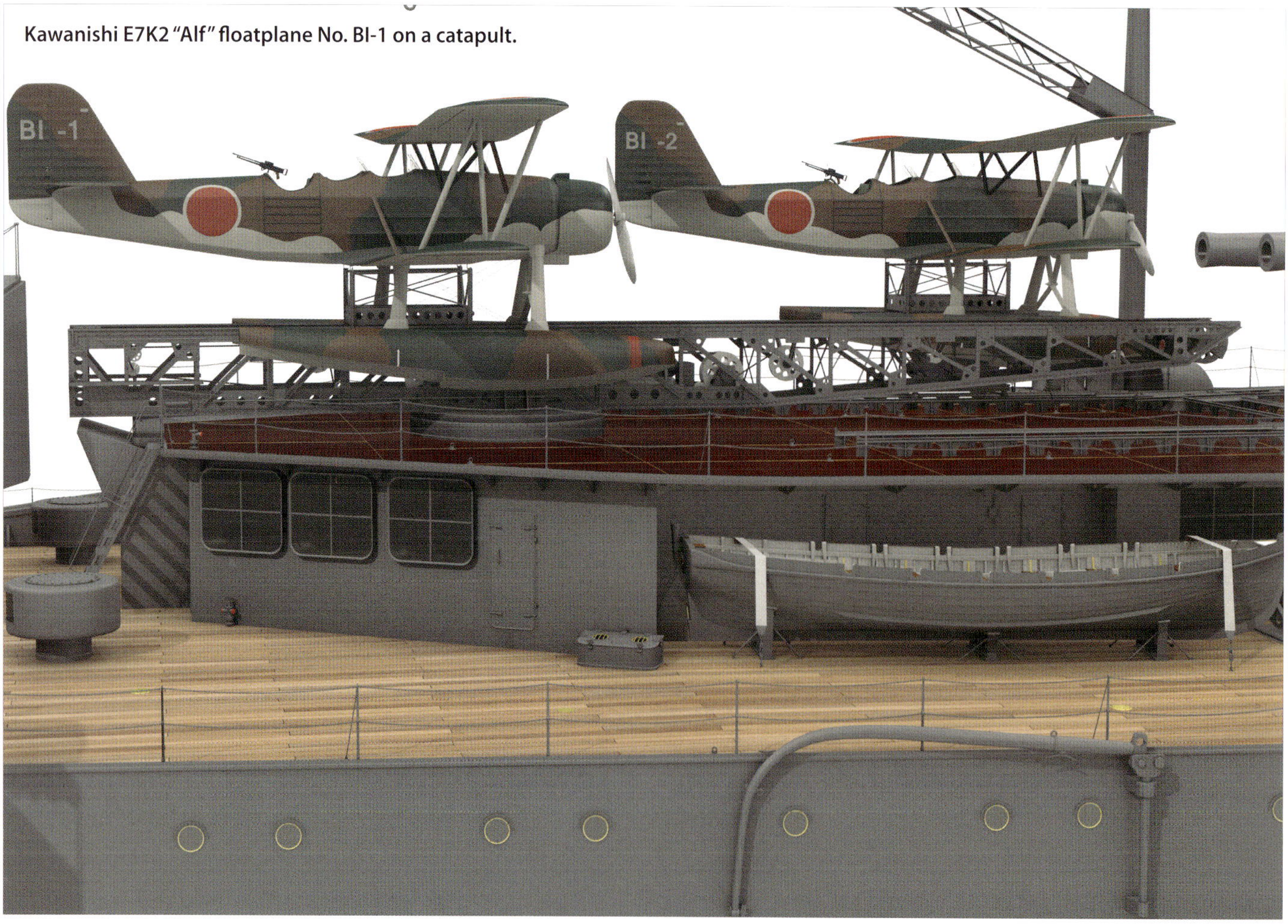

Kawanishi E7K2 "Alf" floatplane No. BI-1 on a catapult.

Kawanishi E7K2 "Alf" floatplanes on the aircraft deck of the battleship.

Bird's eye view of the Kawanishi E7K2 "Alf" floatplanes on the aircraft deck.

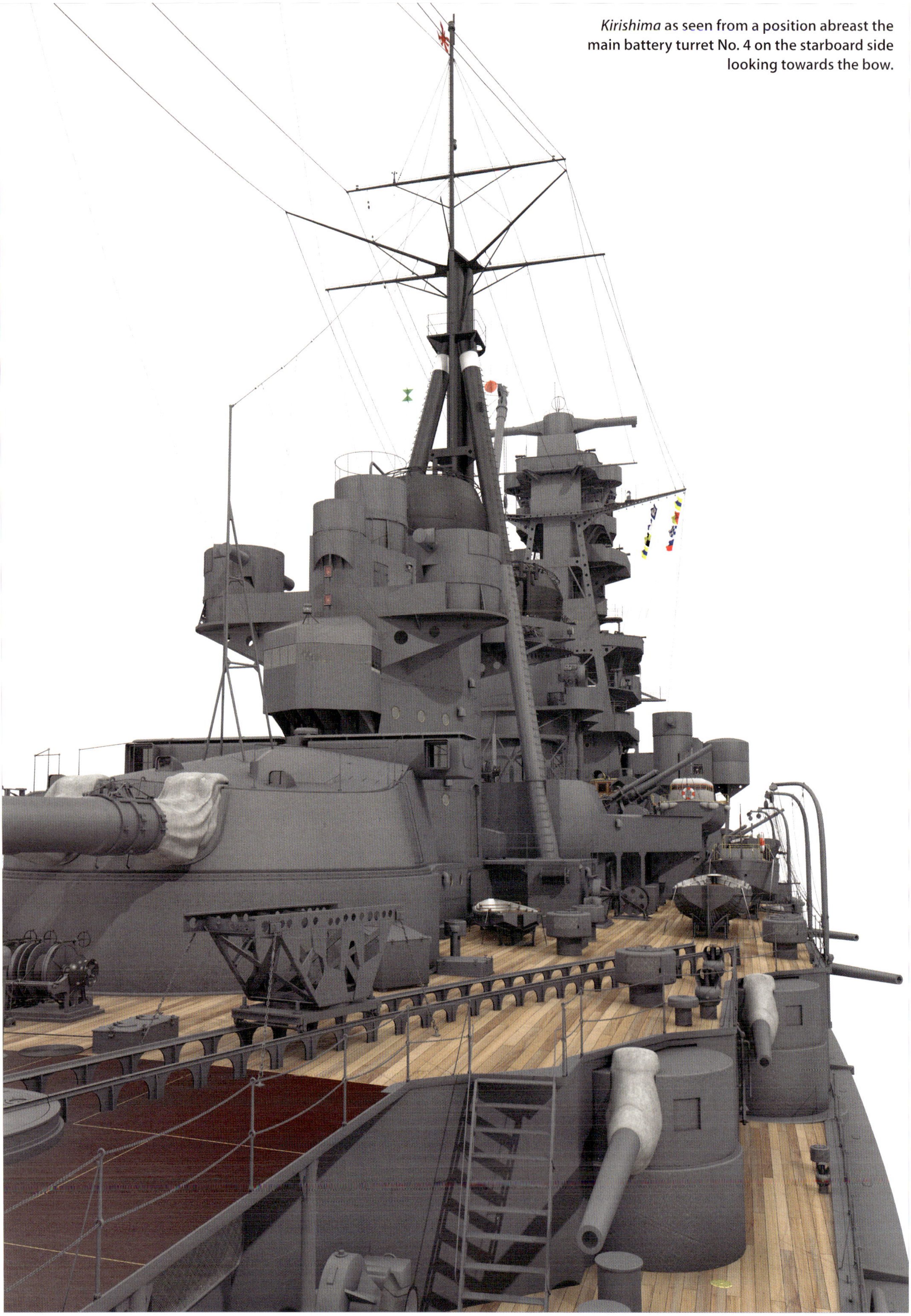

Kirishima as seen from a position abreast the main battery turret No. 4 on the starboard side looking towards the bow.

Starboard side of the quarterdeck. A 9-metre life boat is clearly visible.

Vents on the starboard side of the barbette of the main battery gun turret No. 4.

Rigged accommodation ladder as seen from the aft superstructure deck.

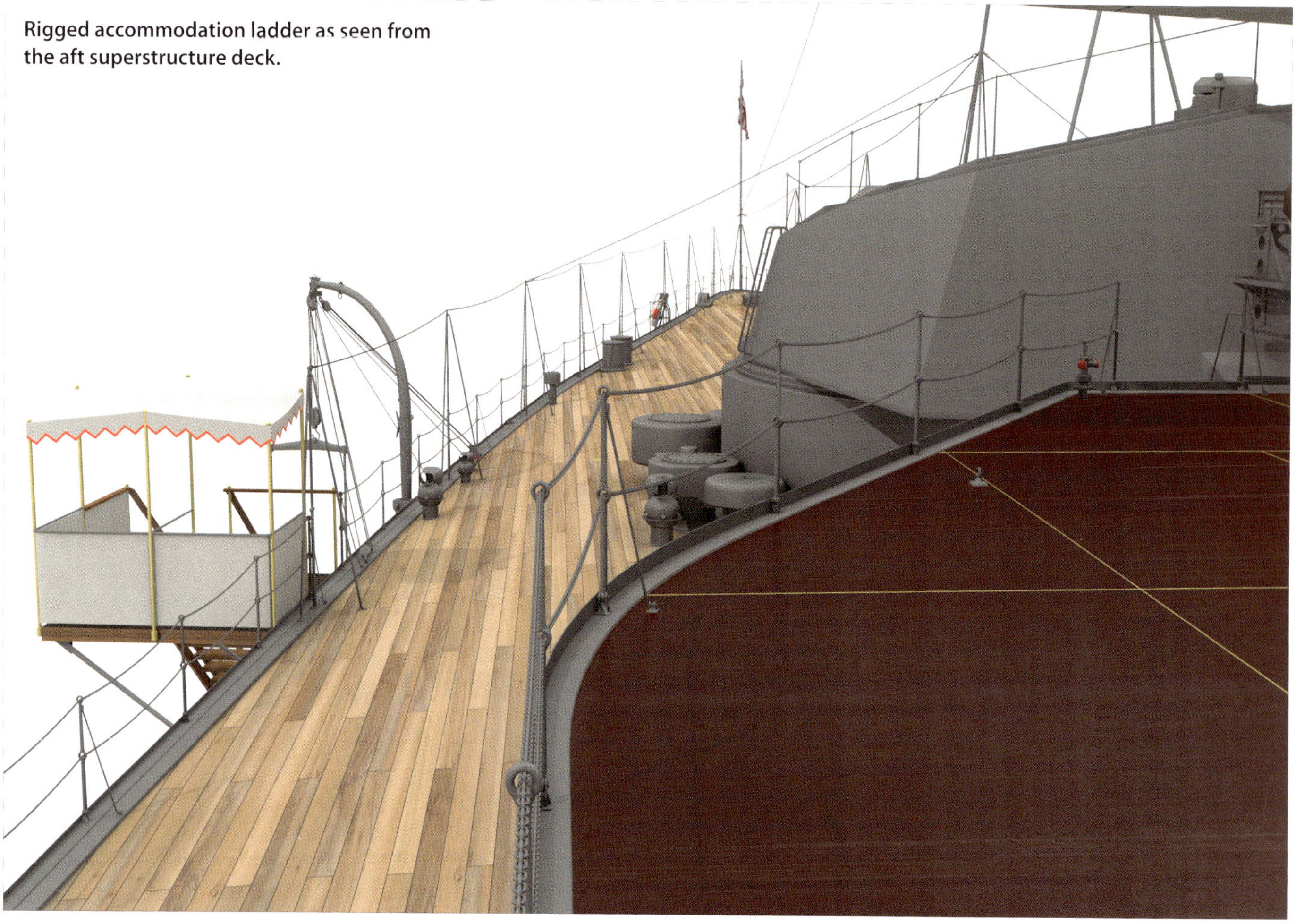

Starboard side aft accommodation ladder.

Rigged accommodation ladder on the starboard side.

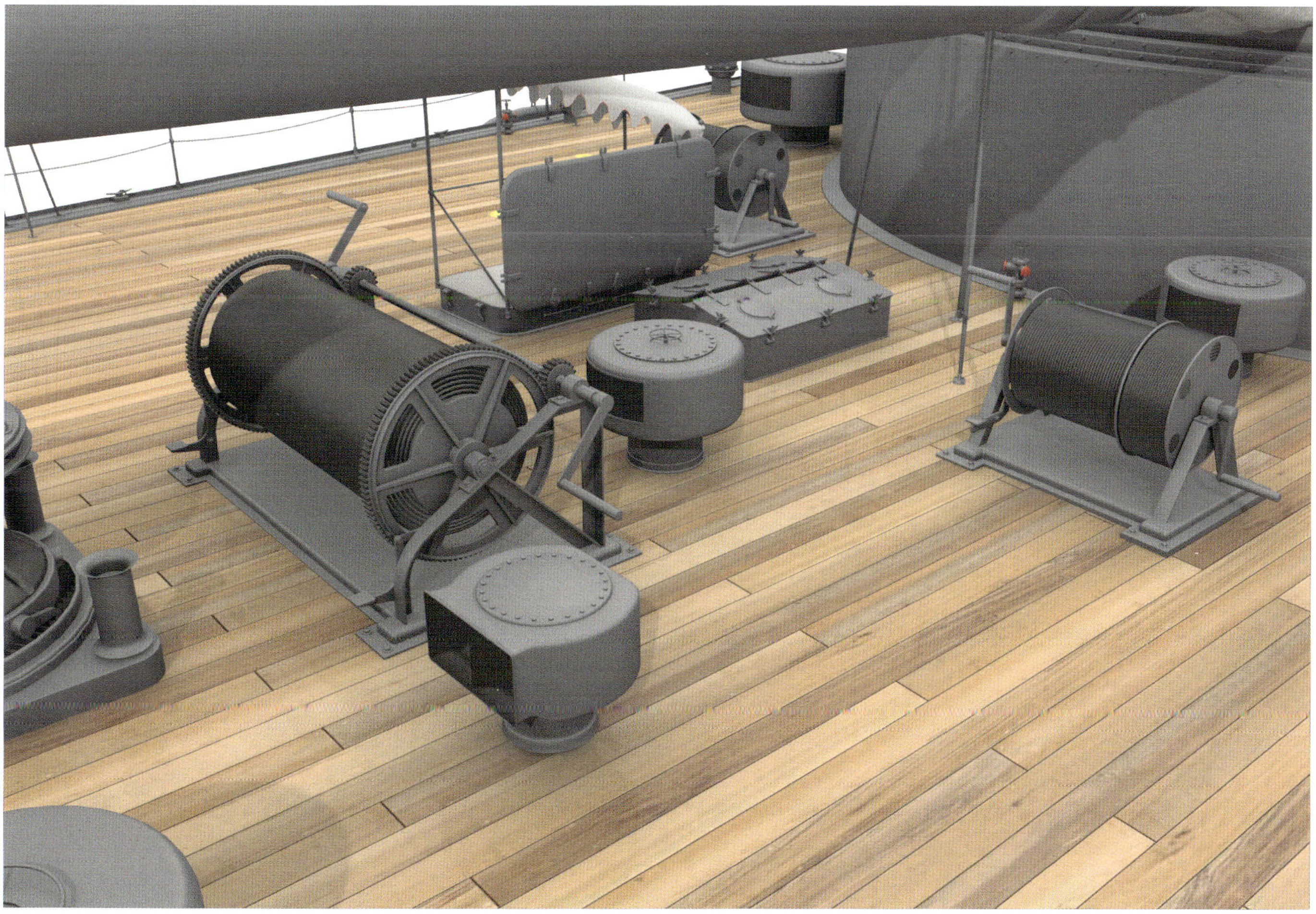

2.2-metre and 1-metre cable reels and deck fittings behind the main battery gun turret No. 4.

Stern of the battleship with the accommodation ladder in rigged position on the starboard side.

Starboard side view of the stern section. Propellers and the rudders are clearly visible.

Stern view with the Imperial Japanese Navy ensign flying from the flagstaff.

Imperial chrysanthemum emblem on the bow of the *Kirishima*.

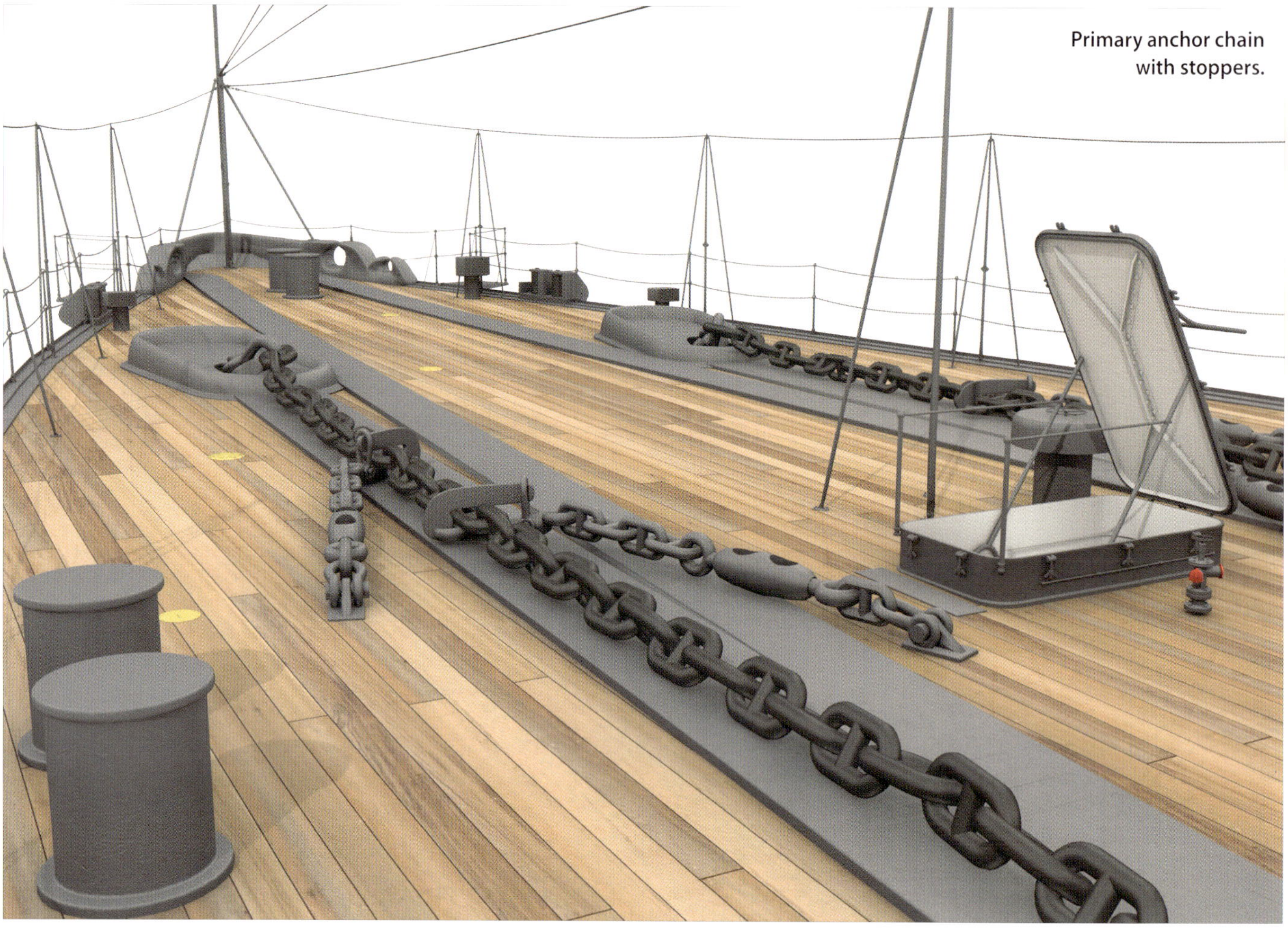

Primary anchor chain with stoppers.

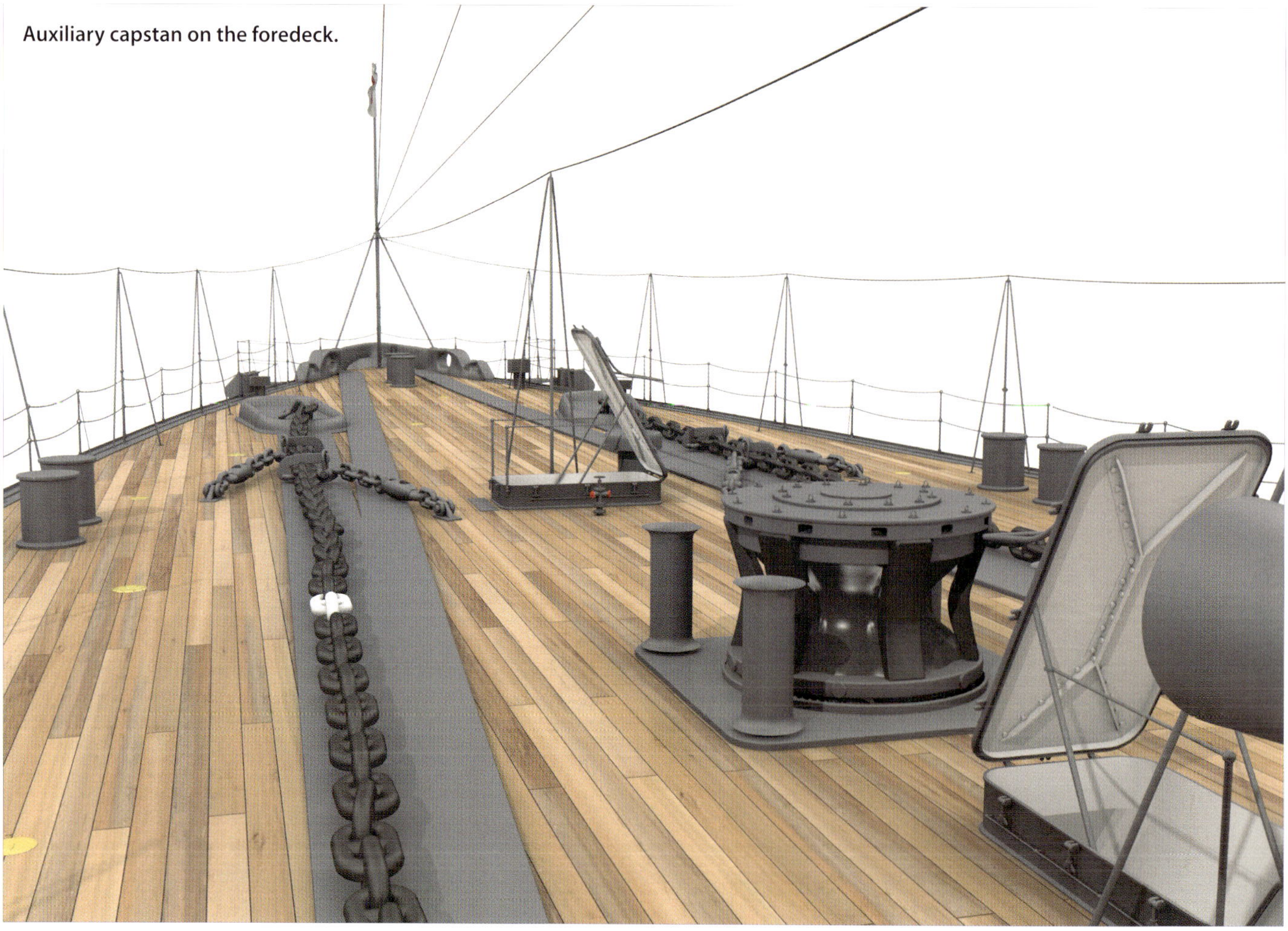

Auxiliary capstan on the foredeck.

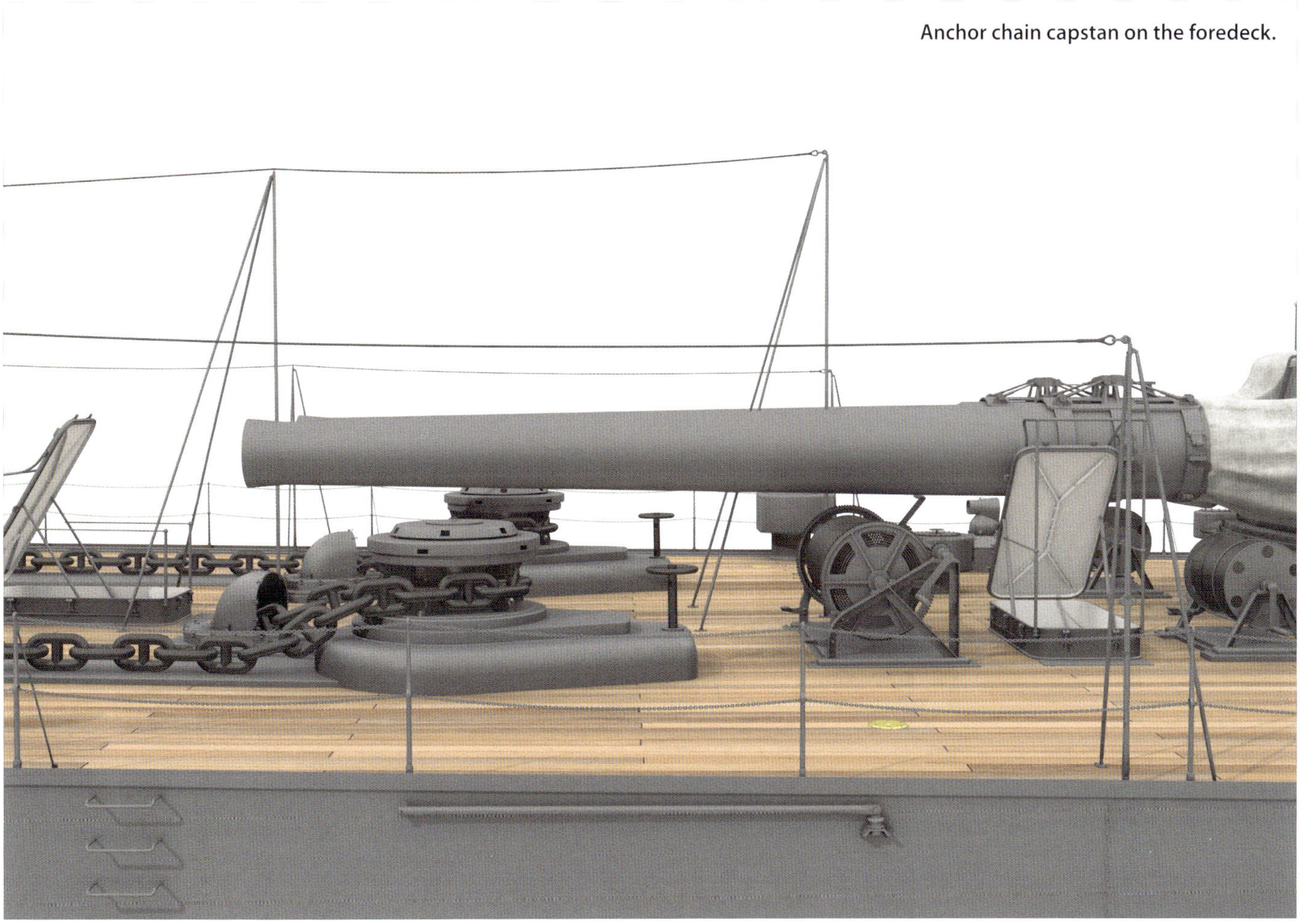
Anchor chain capstan on the foredeck.

Cable reels, vents and a hatch on the foredeck in front of the main battery gun turret No.1.

Main battery gun turret No. 2 with the superstructure in the background.

Main battery gun turret No. 2, similarly to turret No. 3, was equipped with an auxiliary rangefinder installed on its roof.

Bridge superstructure in all its glory as seen from the port side.

A view of the base of the bridge superstructure on the starboard side. Various fittings, paravane gear and 8-metre sampan are visible.

Port side observation platform abreast the base of the bridge superstructure.

Base of the bridge superstructure as seen from the port side.

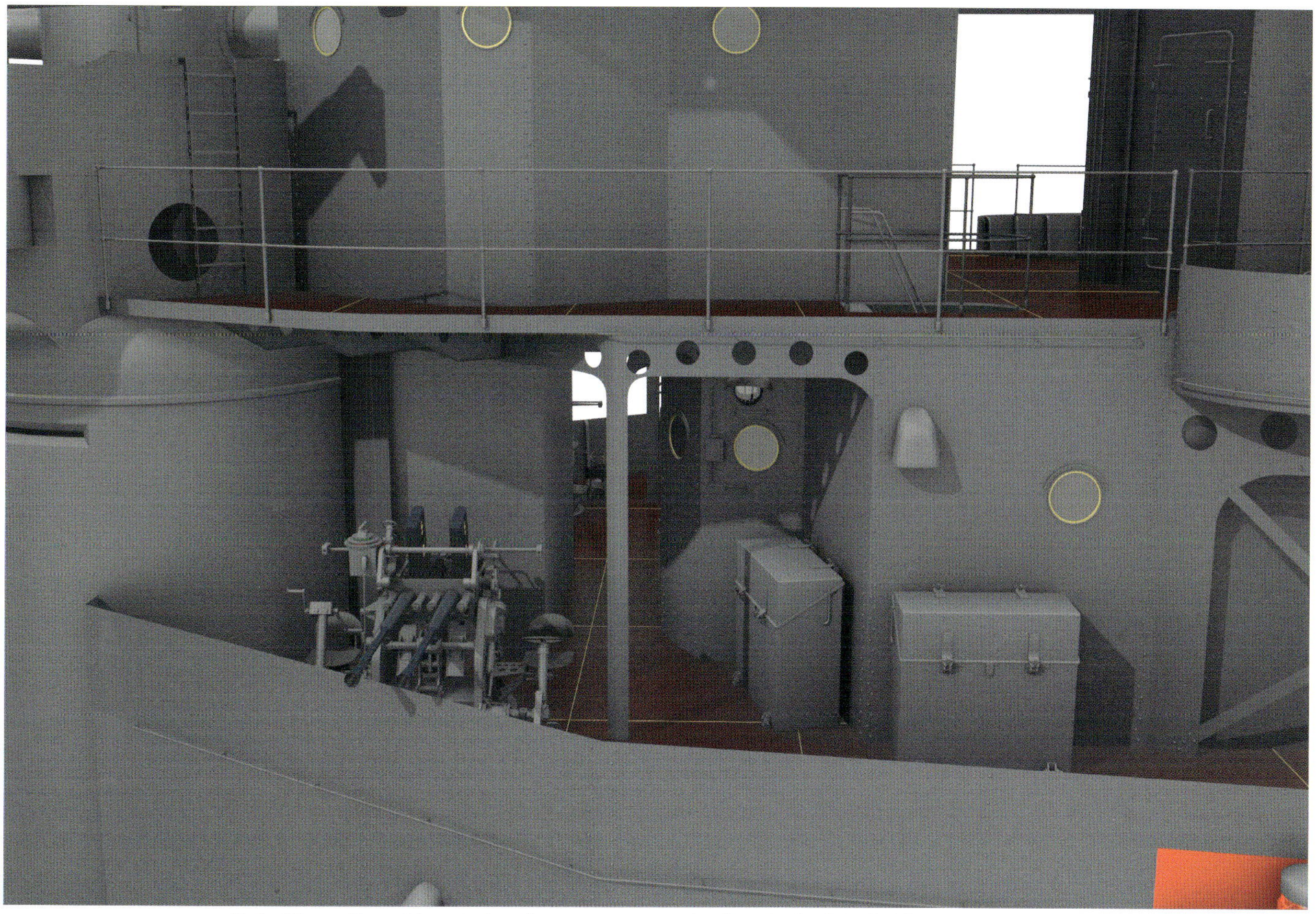

Twin 25 mm Type 96 anti-aircraft gun mount on the first deck of the bridge superstructure.

View from the upper decks of the bridge superstructure at a twin 25 mm MG Type 96 anti-aircraft gun mounted on its first deck.

Two twin 25 mm Type 96 anti-aircraft guns on the fore platform of the bridge superstructure. A 4.5-metre rangefinder can be seen behind the starboard side gun mount.

Main battery gun turrets No. 1 and No.2 on the foredeck. The port side 4.5-metre rangefinder installed on the side of the twin 25 mm Type 96 anti-aircraft gun platform located on the front face of the bridge superstructure is visible.

Rangefinder, 60 cm searchlight and a twin 25 mm Type 96 gun mount on the observation deck of the bridge superstructure.

Observation and auxiliary posts on the port side upper decks of the bridge superstructure.

110 cm searchlights on platforms around the funnel.

A twin 25 mm Type 96 anti-aircraft gun mount on the observation deck of the bridge superstructure.

Decks of the bridge superstructure.

Signal deck.

Signalling flag post in the back of the bridge superstructure.

Ladder leading from the deck of the bridge superstructure to the port side observation post.

Port side observation and 4.5-metre rangefinder posts.

The back of the bridge superstructure with the port side observation posts.

Boat deck behind the bridge superstructure.

Deck behind the bridge structure with the cable reels, electric winches and the stored wood used for quick damage repairs.

9-metre cutter on the port side davits.

Port side 17-metre motor pinnace – ceremonial barge and a 12-metre motor launch with a 9-metre cutter stowed on top of it.

Starboard side twin 25 mm Type 96 anti-aircraft gun mounted in the midship section.

Midship section as seen from the port side. A twin 25mm Type 96 anti-aircraft gun mount is visible.

First funnel with 110 cm searchlights platforms.

First funnel as seen from the stern.

Secondary battery 15.2 cm guns in the port side casemates.

Boom for handling ship boats in a stored position.

View of the midship section with the boom used for handling the ship boats in a stowed position.

Port side view of the bridge superstructure and the midship section.

Port side midship. The rails for handling the 13-metre landing boat are visible.

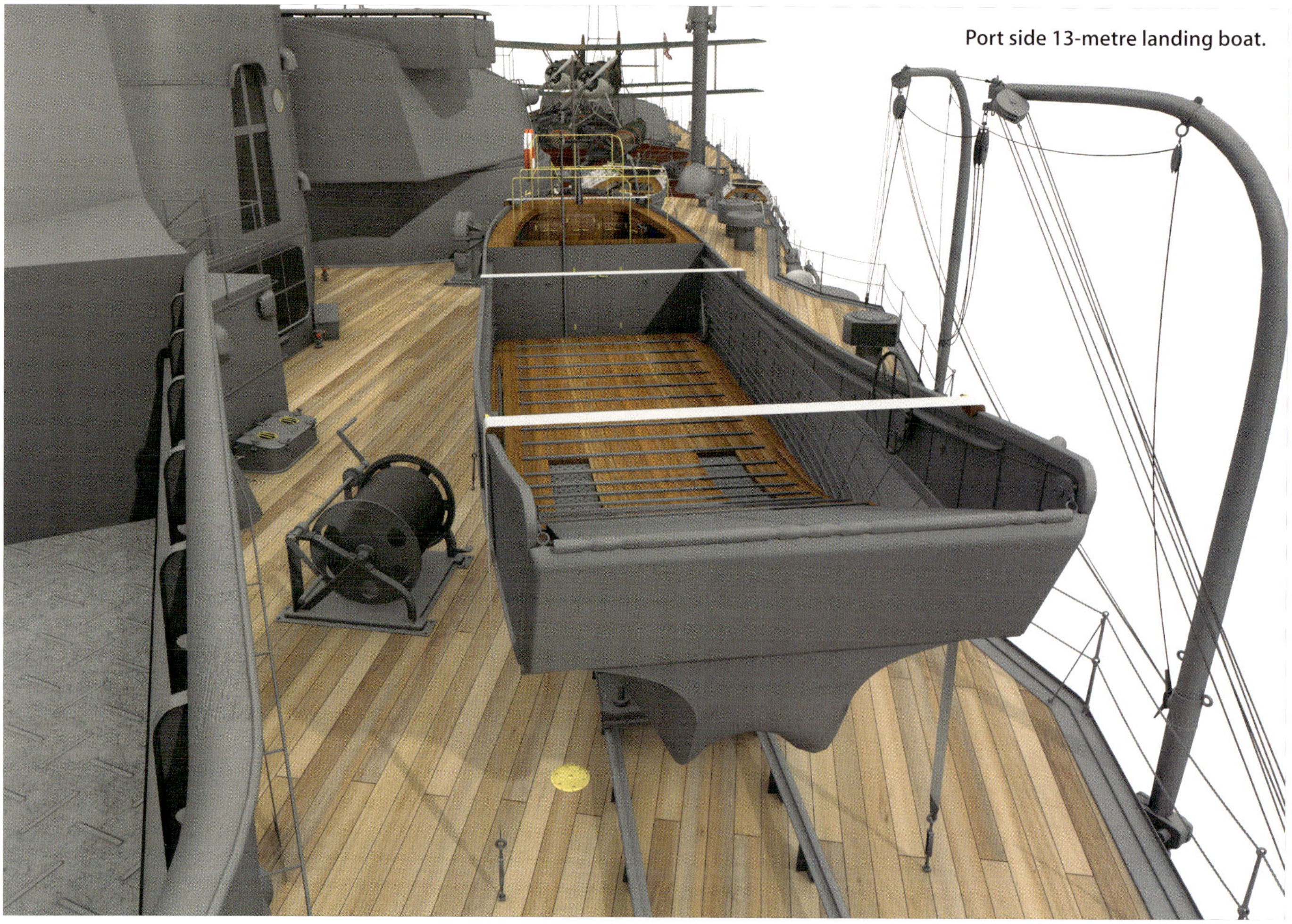

Port side 13-metre landing boat.

Steam winch powering the boom for handling the ship boats.

Twin 25mm Type 96 anti-aircraft gun mountings on the platforms between the legs of the mainmast.

The head of the mainmast.

Second funnel.

Second funnel and aft superstructure as seen from the port side.

Stern section as seen from the port side.

Midship section.

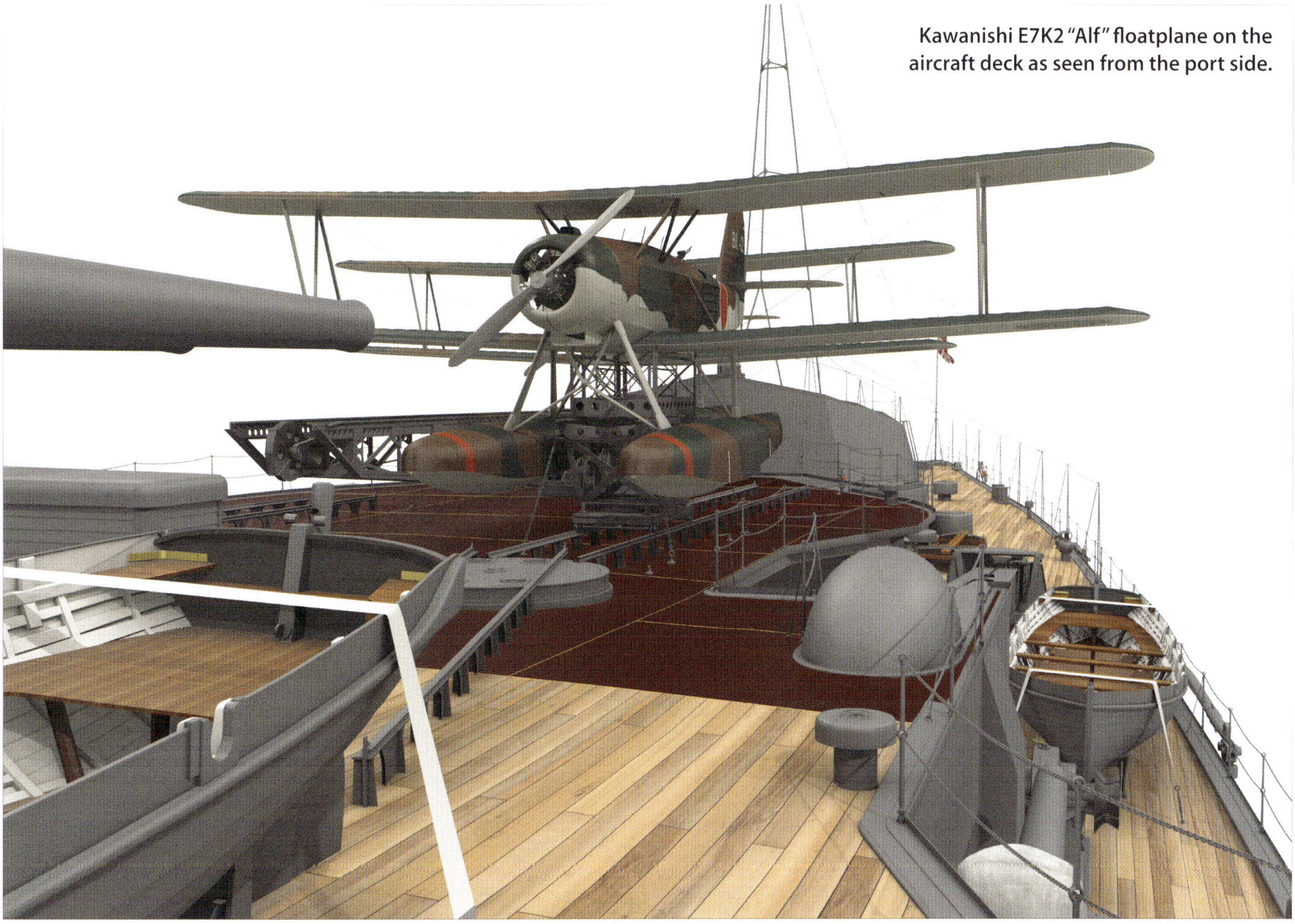

Kawanishi E7K2 "Alf" floatplane on the aircraft deck as seen from the port side.

Steam winch located behind the barbette of the main battery gun turret No. 3. The rails used for moving around the floatplanes are visible and the floatplane trolley can be seen in the background.

Port side midship section as seen from astern.

Port side secondary battery 15.2 cm guns in aft casemates.

Main battery turret No. 2 located in front of the aircraft deck, similarly to turret No. 2, was equipped with auxiliary rangefinder.

Aircraft deck and the stern section.

Kawanishi E7K2 "Alf" floatplanes on the port side section of the aircraft deck.

The crane for handling floatplanes in the stowed position.

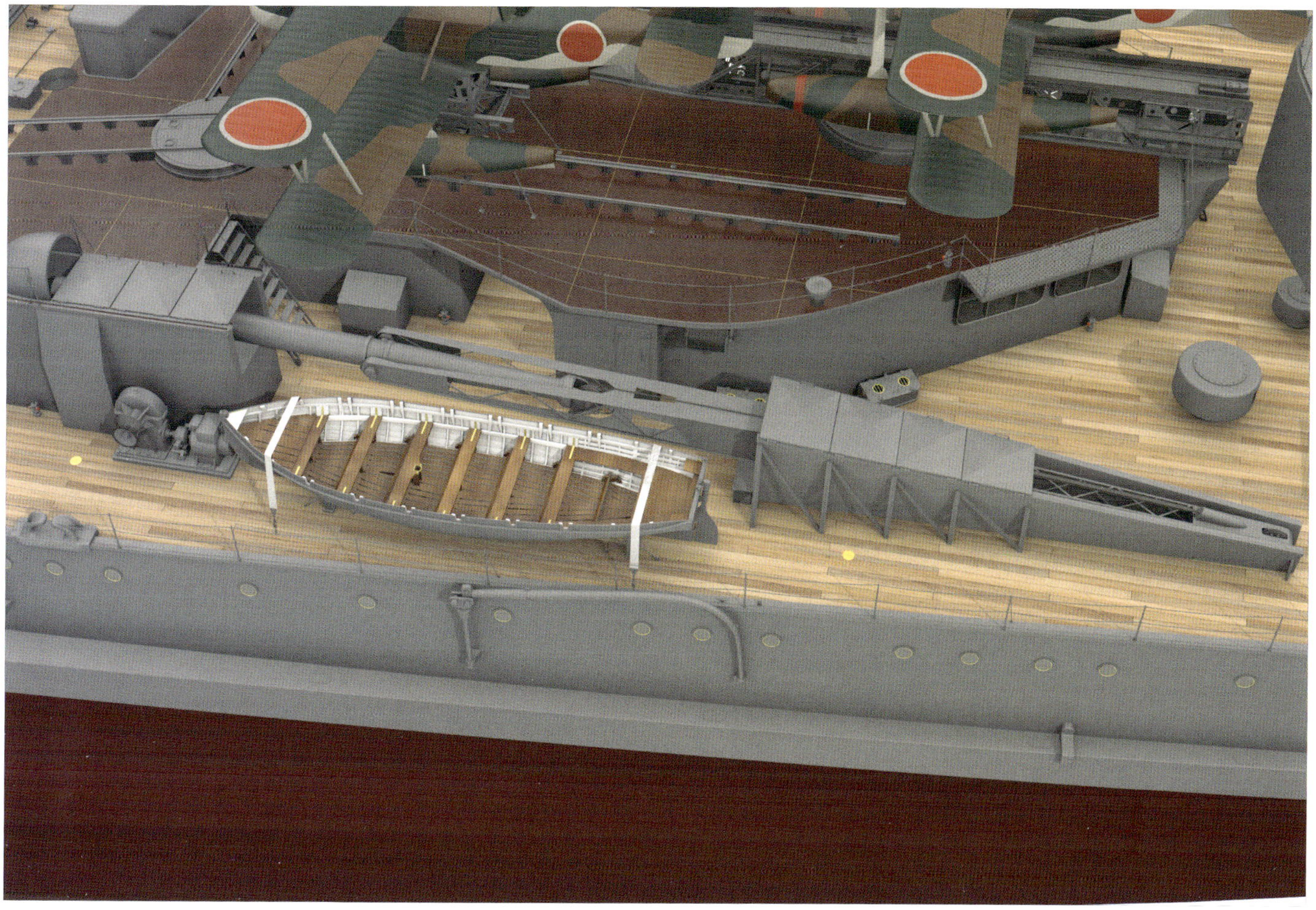

The crane for handling aircraft in a stowed position.

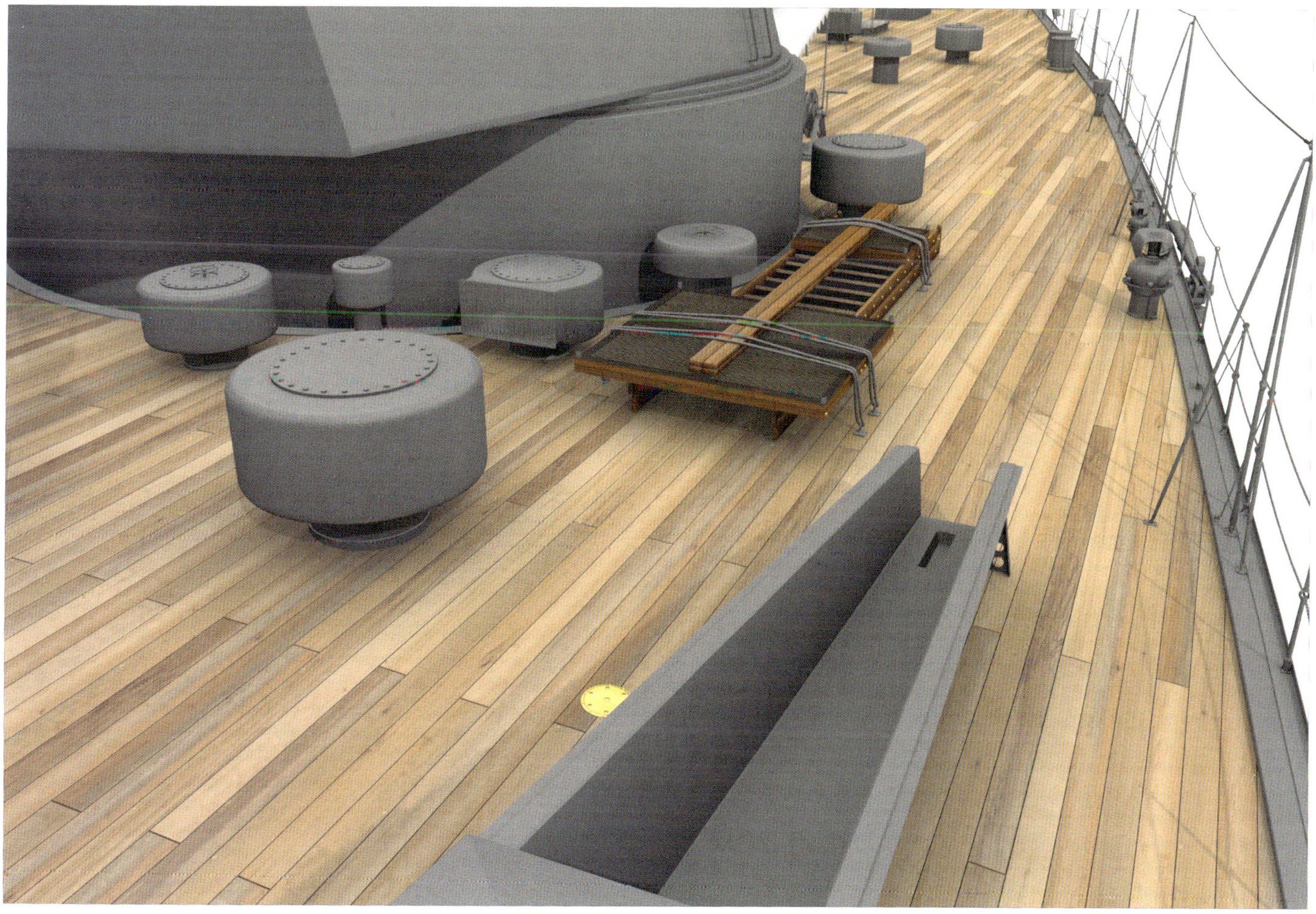

Stowed accommodation ladder abreast main battery gun turret No. 4.

Main battery turret No. 4 on the quarterdeck.

Quarterdeck of the battleship as seen from a position abreast the main battery gun turret No.4.

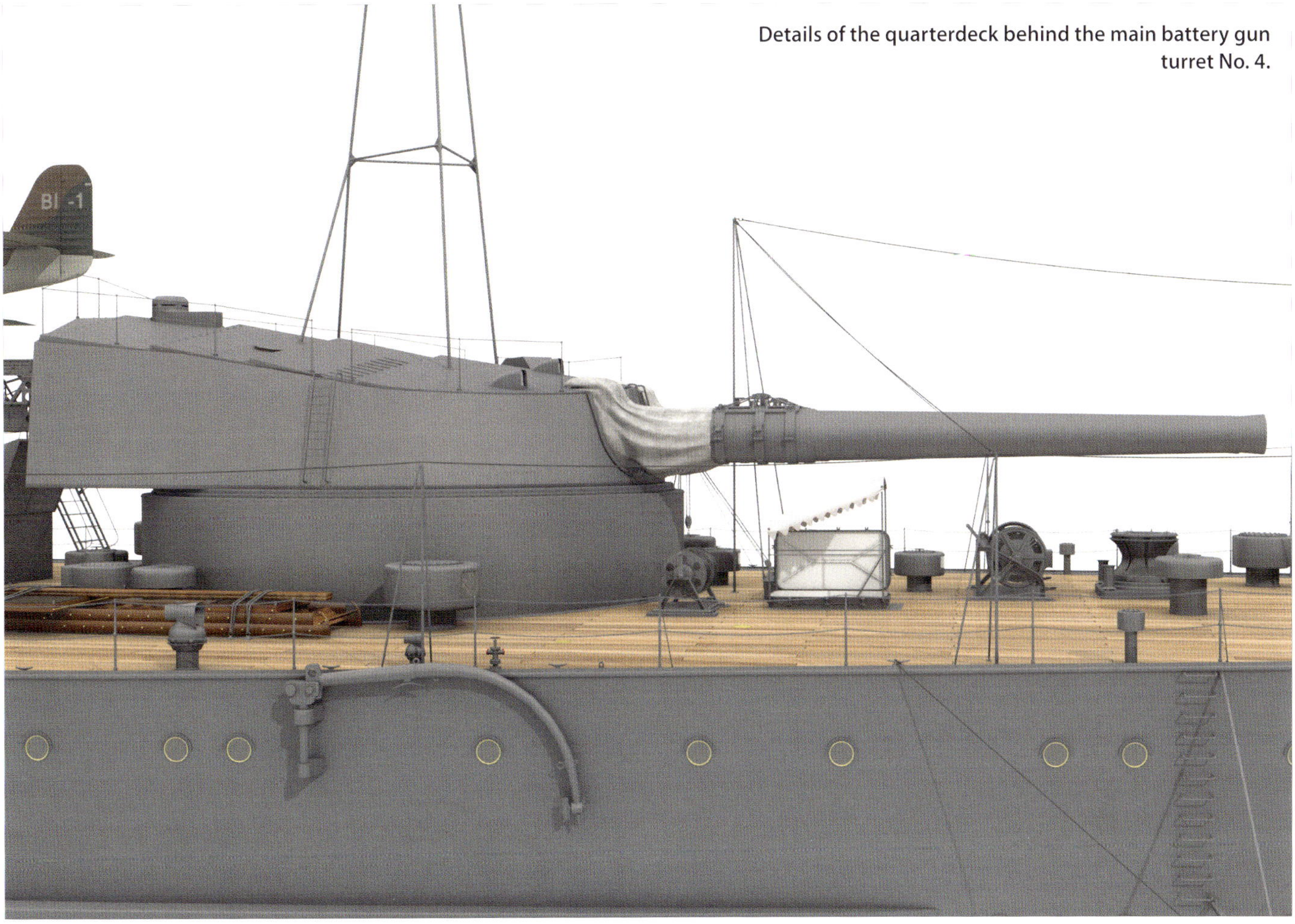

Details of the quarterdeck behind the main battery gun turret No. 4.

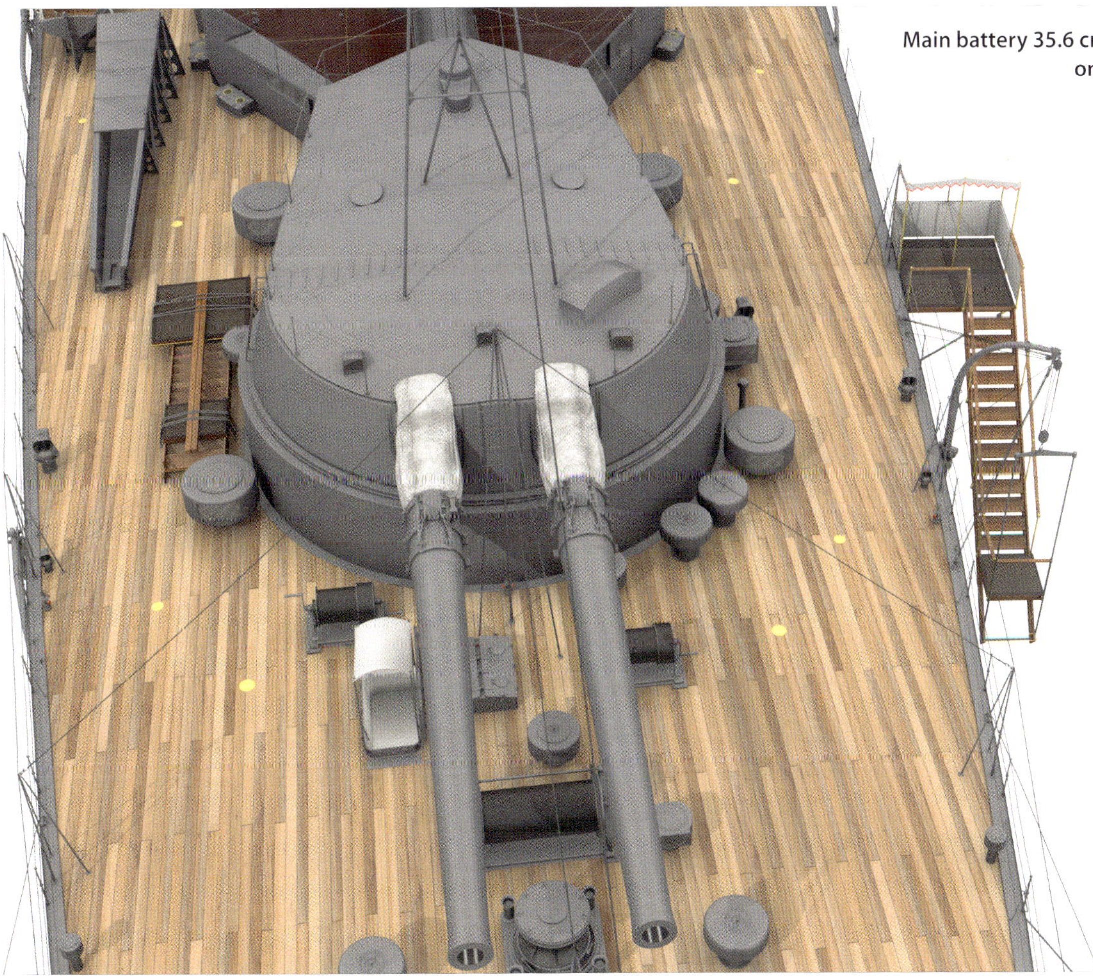
Main battery 35.6 cm gun turret No. 4 on the quarterdeck.

Main battery gun turret No.4 on the quarterdeck.

Quarterdeck hatch.

Port side stern anchor with the folding propeller guard protecting the propeller.

Quadruple skylights on the quarterdeck.

Aft quadruple skylights.

Life ring and the flagstaff with the Imperial Japanese Navy ensign.

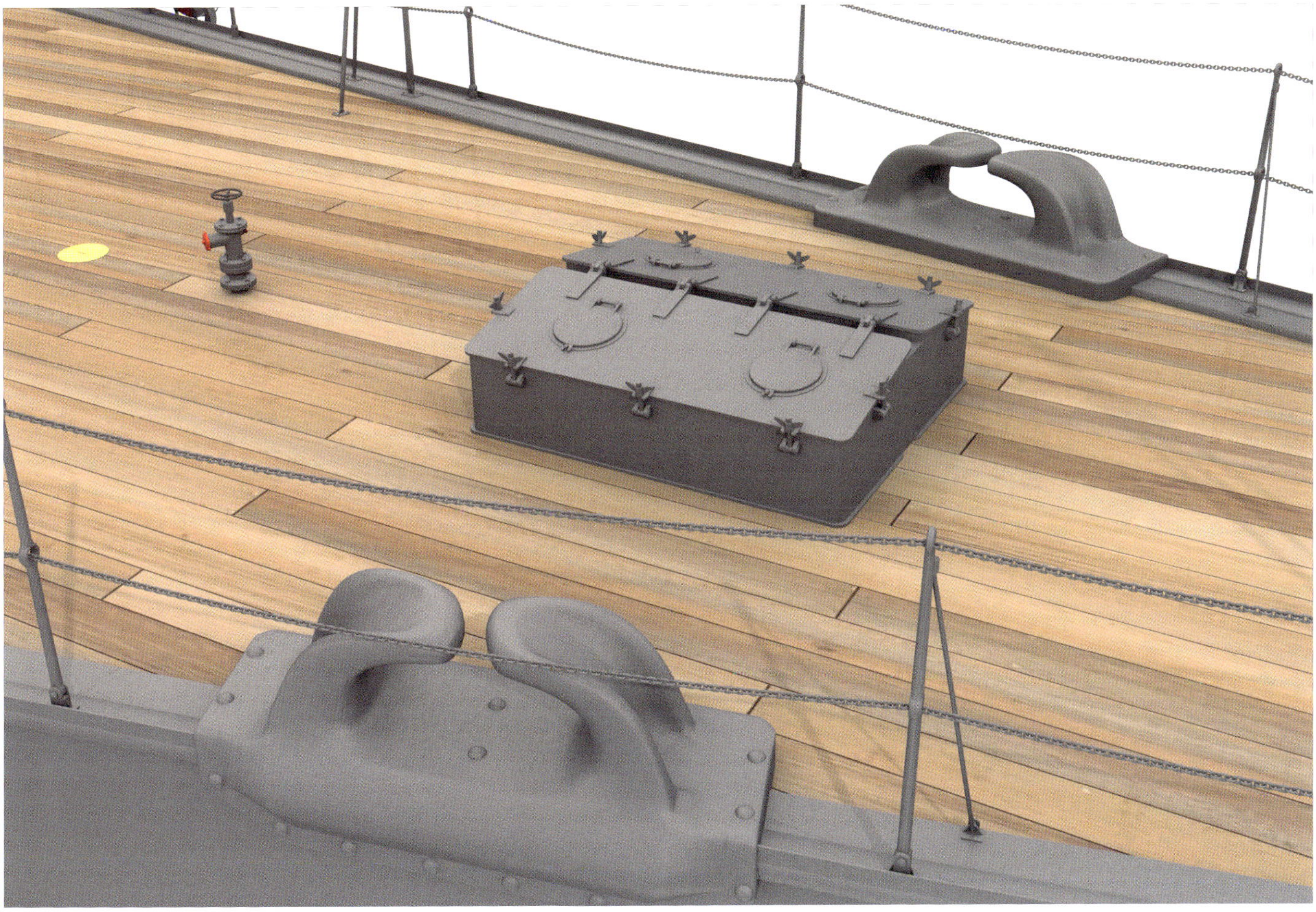

Double skylights on the quarterdeck.

Kirishima as seen from a position at the end of the quarterdeck.

Kirishima at anchor.

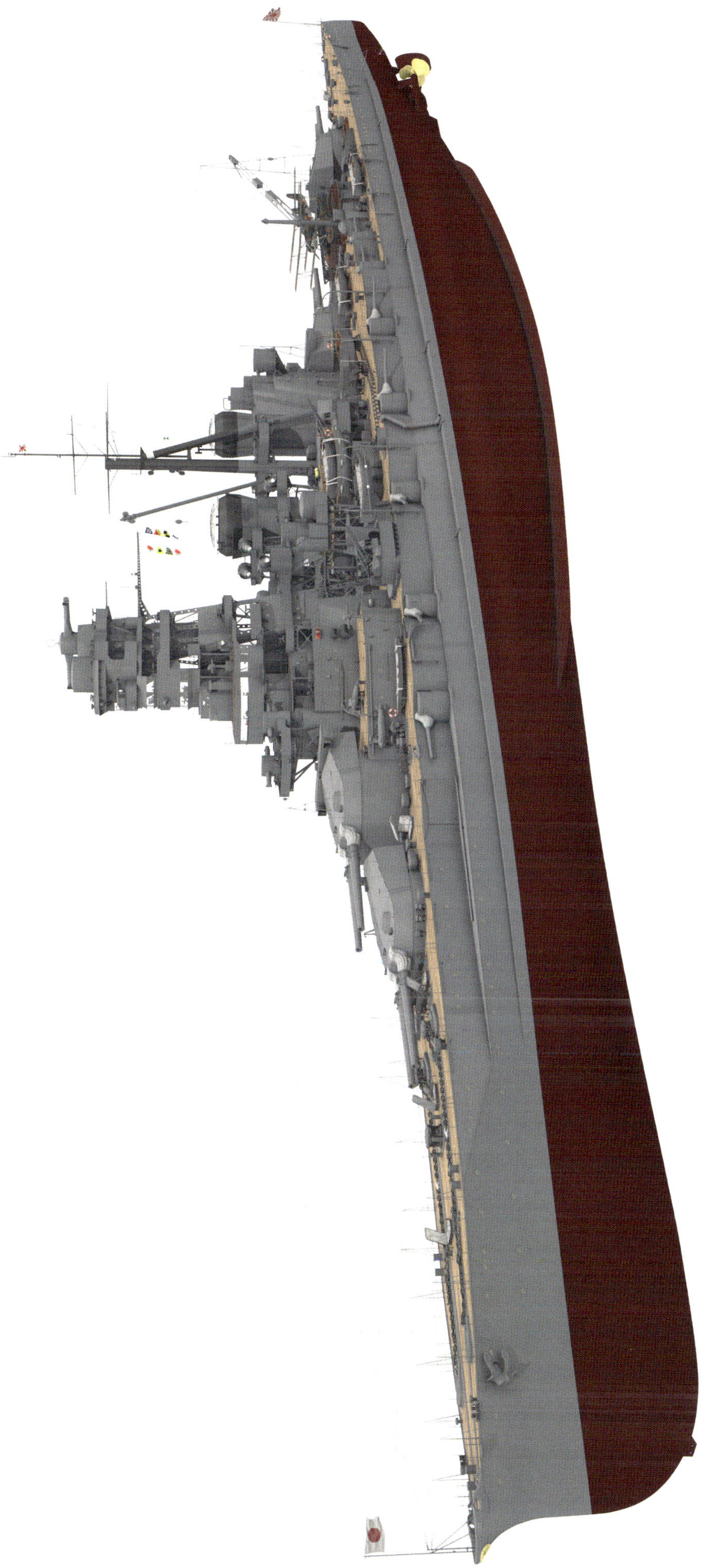

The Japanese Battleship *Kirishima* 1940.

The Japanese Battleship Kirishima 1940 – Waldemar Góralski
LUBLIN 2019 • ISBN 978-83-66148-59-8

3D illustrations and captions: **Waldemar Góralski** • Text: **Piotr Wiśniewski** • Translation: **Kazimierz Zygadło (captions), Tomasz Basarabowicz (text)** • Design: **KAGERO STUDIO** – Łukasz Maj
KAGERO Publishing • www.kagero.pl, e-mail: kagero@kagero.pl, marketing@kagero.pl
Editorial office, Marketing, Distribution: KAGERO Publishing, Akacjowa 100, os. Borek, Turka, 20-258 Lublin 62, Poland, phone/fax (+48) 81 501 21 05
www.kagero.eu

3D visualisations are based on the available photographs, drawings and other archive data, and should be treated only as author's attempt to recreate the original look of the particular machine as faithfully as possible. If you are in possession of materials to which author did not reach, and you would like to help us to develop a better publication, please contact the Publisher on: redakcja@kagero.pl